Quaternity

Scott Glassman
&
Sheila E. Murphy

Otoliths

Quaternity by Scott Glassman & Sheila E. Murphy

Copyright © 2009 by
Scott Glassman & Sheila E. Murphy

Cover design by K.S.Ernst & Sheila E. Murphy

Cover preparation by harry k stammer

ISBN: 978-0-9806025-1-7

Printed in the U.S.A.

Otoliths
8 Kennedy St
Rockhampton
QLD 4700
Australia

http://stores.lulu.com/l_m_young
http://the-otolith.blogspot.com

For Beverly Carver and Sanford Glassman

I falter before the task of finding the language which might adequately express the incalculable paradoxes of love.

- Carl Jung

The authors are grateful to editors of the following publications
in which segments of this book first appeared:

Jacket, EOAGH, Shadowtrain, and *The Duplications*.

1.

Magenta works alone, surrounded by ripe worlds
pinned also to labels, and the labels own the land.
Until yesterday, indifference resided in blood veins.

Whoever intended to answer, rose, isolated, frozen in
chicory groves, turquoise-fed, chlorinated: *it wasn't the sea*
eyelight's blasé gourd-prim shatterproof hour, coagulating.

Tintype drew the senses to a brittle path, minced sticks
melded with crushed stone as if the way were at once rigid
and hand-drawn flexing an all-gray revue of granularity.

Scope contaminates moth-eaten cursives, pleating
each flame, orphan of chord; beeline's symmetrical curl
chafes in quartz, percussive blues, wet strychnine pews.

Conditioned lure of foreground tames both quarter horse
and values [core] canonical url detailing Orpheus
a-strum leaking the myth of recent stems in truth.

The crinoline "do not look back" perforates contact highs
its dioxides fervently mean imminence, "devices"
per se (lock) syncopated wedding bands for Prada flotation.

Lops ided coin toss extricates the innocence from romance
occipital in (f)lux (drawn lace) priced wincing in drumbeat(en)
patch of status quatrains severing the curfew from the cuffs.

Youth-poised plink of failsafe Portia echoing leaves
lotion's syllabic best-of-all possibly incarnated fauna
where art dowries too squelch the umlaut into shape.

Laudate simmers oddly, working in mindful affection
close to chapel of happenstance endowing
the après-midi with faun's rhapsodic pitch parfait.

As in the midst, in the midst of midsts, in the midst
of missing midsts, amidst the palpitation, a junta breeds
pronominal props and polo'd rainforests clapping shut.

A rapidity of castings leashes back quashed spores
remanded to the divvying of losses once thought
core now juxtaposed with an informal winter.

Spectrum tinsels the ready-made floes to a liking
of distance, particled purse pretty one day as onyx
takes its crystalline into breath and overture, as thirst.

What is the first thing shaded when a bud splits open?
Pebbles, shards, low weather miming the read-only
chime(ra) choicing see-through sieves of reverie.

Siren's plasticity hungers for chronology *au revoir*
mon cherie puréed obelisk "night" reverberates on
staccato, or at fault, serenaded coldly by the fractal "I".

Softening the sky, a *laissez-faire* motif effaces
self in favor of convivial montage, erasing the faux
chilly brass ascension into plural depths.

Elopement: lint-fire vestibules, camphoric wings
contracting mosaic's latitudinal collisions, pier-scraped
pastures ballooning to the size of June's gentrified myth.

Place to park refutes a rumored traction, tap shoes
shelved beside lint wings have gathered old
attention, co-motion ceasing (to make sense).

Moth-buckled ozones are pantries, rust-vacant shelter
laces kerosene, widens scant portals of encounter *has it
ever occurred* bruises twilight scattering its low-lit ivories.

Fault follows *no,* as incantation bests the helter
of ace vents made once clean, giving a wide berth
ides of ruses lit with vortices come Celtic sips of port.

Myrrh shudders metronomically (spilled) inundated yolks
quotas annotated concentrations excrete sleep-pollen-briny
hulls burn off Napa morning (ferments) its prodigal nocturne.

Prompt warmth rises to the polls as nightly vindication of the May dance just concluding centerful
and wined down pastures parting the rinds tossed into urns.

Vanishing the elliptical, unto is undone, "was" wants back in
the celebratory plash *yonder ye olde* inscrutable nebulae
capstone whip-poor-wills hem weeping how-why algaes ebb.

Regulations (reams) stiffen amid Dionysian sprees
continually minting new panache to rival an incumbent
cache of devotees uplifting hems left to ellipses.

Layer: epileptic i-before-e parenthesis hurls accents event-
death razes the tower basket born already, crawlspace clings
wells red-brick instant (vaccine) trysts adhere to blackout.

Forth | with | holds. Capiche? Trauma's made eventual by virtue
of the chanting function, Extreme Unction, fly-bys made
to seem as unplanned as the easing of darkness via brackets, via fence.

No tú sabes co-in ci -dent cuando mi nombre for accidental-logues whose
pyrrhic drift empiric al -ly tidy :: para las almas y noirish capitulated rosedroop
where (what) rain binds (by) telepathic Tarot wand whispers down V-neck lilith.

Shhh: she sleepeth. And the driven sidelines shuck the width of skies'
skittery almas drifting to sunlit piemen piecemealing flavory wafers under the
stirs' tested triple chances blind to teleprisms' lavish paragram of toasty noir.

Chrome self perspires loaves regardless of meadow parallels. Sleep is another
carcass for daylight folly and long-necked highway tryptophan shifts its
l'chaim floodland schism's normal growth[2] "fa-so-la" realities anhedonic as
firefly moons.

Tepidity re-merges a delinquent posse of mead throats low-waying through
landfills parallel to rowboats earning headway by attending to the slither
of shrinking liquid norms so long as empirical roaming charges don't apply.

Belonging to whom: after all / some / nothing. Necktie electrifies strangulation
rhythms. Disposal is grated, collected as triangulated coins, the backside each
summit forgets. Stained-glass pyramids mortify one another for Nile or
Skuykill coteries in roomy ovens.

Loaves of loves deride an ounce of dispensation tainted by ventricular slide. Commandments mortared to the brain elongate pain time while canaries flicker amid rate wars, debate chores, conglomerate style sheets and pilfered scuffings.

Parsonage is personage, counting debacles up to the dendrite hilt, decades (lit) inexactly gored. The toppled frieze wants its visitors to expedite this diffusion of glandular responsibility hours resurfacing their eyes for secular red-light rollback exaltations.

Contrition s/talks the guilty eye. An expeditious journey seems to ratchet up the spine to meet the sense (of sight). Fusion tilts spondees until red rock jilts feigners from a poke town surfaced with the nibs of debs in traction vis-à-vis a weightless spice.

500 deserts on the fritz cirrus rain sprouts unelected. Perniciously blind an urchin groans on mute (oceans cultivate a rapture for iodized / harmonics / infancy). Foreigner galaxy-crafts belly up to "acolytes of flux" yadda yadda boom! jo bang-motion hijacks fjords.

Spills blind the closely held desert floor infantilized by foreign cherishing. A blimp goes by. Alarm-fed visuals luxuriate in rapt poise as if and only if the boombox were not shattering the nearness of the lexicon of flesh breath typified by lulls in quilting.

Heliopolis of Hindenburg naps in periodical Damascus-burn diminutia (-olition) as viola commas include fiery exit-omniscience. They register at 20/50 three times Fahrenheit's apple-a-day reproval. Squab snivels to unearth a scarab's stony cylindrical appendix.

Omni-practice brains the proven cinderquake as trauma sprains fertility into chrysanthemum's own blossy little takes. Awake pomade! Your op-cit fire emits the fracas we've been waning for to shout at golf across a person's penury.

Afterscruff bevels coy foundations rotting stardate chemistry to a wish. Pen-ultimate-ferry cutoff sh-u-n-s the ardent freon world and sees what good restricts / raises abstinence (-ence) how it appears to end every hole-in-one capsule: blood's heuristic.

Chemlab charms the argent out of deep pock(et)s of the prince gone coy
by stricture, nabbing poultice from the see-sawn brittle wool meant to scuff
choices from surface and to form smoothness tangibly perceived.

Dementia questions entirety salmon's risk the lake foal and by depth
screeches something the pebble wheel conceives on Friday flipped
on its tonsil temptress ovaled ostrich examples crimp the water whines.

Deciduous meantime trees void sap from the competing shimmy of some listless breezy needles(s) in opacity drippling along lippy oleolike oomph
as heel to toe tire tenders sill-top while an individual reads Sillitoe.

Arguably cowardice cowers to the fillerup brim lunar diana-phone, oxygen
turning dry brush to the floor of mountainous distraction distraction it is all
a finish matte olay! dip to ice depreciate the impetuous sayonara signage.

Philippic tiles crash to the cement floor as if to shore up scars
in motional rush to turn phonetics into dicey tissue via petulant
cribbage games turned southerly after dipstick triage points to a defection.

~

Parsimony referees the tremulous butterfly cottage. Bones heal a quicksand
effluvia scampering to noun and quota. The ante rises on a plume of gypsum.
Direction is a humidity, false shapes resounding stand, stammer, take refuge.

Depiction white leaves pressed once yield archival off-tones veering
toward a yellow mid-cast on a tough board that shows the butterflies. As
happens, sounds allow revering of the wings that plume their way toward
sand.

Flutter attaches to exploited cure grinds among planetrees acting
nonchalant versus beach eroding its passenger dread that those
who come all gripped with skin aren't as passive as the flippant apex.

Decode me when you're free of read things, rippling against active *voici*
lingering along each ploy abutting rinds left in chalets we tacked on
to our holdings reasoning that fact-finding would shed few kin.

There is yew (you) an under-the-radar debutante girder swaying over
volcanic grist, lines as wet syllables fold in and die, the fire grazing
your face as you confer with its interference and lightning softens poise.

As often as a wish comes to negate the actual, fire mutes the folds
along a face half recognized, half forgotten, as the fractions are
conferred upon the rational debate between positions grazing the midline.

Is meaning contraband, arc, organic apostrophe mingling as much in
fetal sarcophagi— what verticality assumes to tempt. Foucault wonders
whether too many Ms arise in mummer to author a trans-sister leap-down.

Lumber's fur remands smooth skin to tabled impositions as onlookers
tingling with positioning subsume neglect into collective cortex and the apex
withers despite risen glands and fervor and adroit leaping to exemption.

How many times does emptiness refuse itself? Redwoods sycamore
grenache cut with Borax adjust their stone tablet arms accordingly, chalk-like
oblongatas (*how we do it* versions of) only taxable as far as nothing.

Cramped confit jams the vision trenched enough to tone the lathered calking
as if medulla were well versed in ax modality with *no* written across *thing*
as though impaginate playthings were enlisted before recognizing sub-stance.

Erector set enervates the let-go landing— all is go is gone is gathered.
Fellowship hacks the brittle centeredness of joy-palated font-sized nettles.
Amygdala, axon-free, jettisons its bastion of stars one per driftlet ounce.

Net wrath in spokes hacks axiology to bits, its vast tar not verve
but trust gone by, once riddled with low ship of epistems braking for
wild spates taller than the lift dest- calling to the voyages amid ontology.

And what of diagrams? Do they appease the lurid O-ring grip to crush
the baby bland? Do geographic accounts as these close their gales on
Wednesdays so the vessel founders deprived of cradle talc and person place-set
as tilt or gash?

Stay the course and blush in alcoves cloves are good for glucose management
talismans shield private spacing talons graph the field of peasants with original
stints made into glands are diacritical endowments play those keys once white.

In the interest of time-elapsed self-administered lilacs, sugar content maximal myofacial clues lead to shredded lisp vacation diaphragm blitzkrieg bluish hens hyping billboard piano strings impressed by dialed-in jockey numbers and neon.

Lucent lead time presses open otherwise numb, lapsed points of glow lensed out of whispered ministrations posed as causal scorching innards of the brackets making speech in tongues a dialup motion blue to touch.

Inscape vibration matches the Planck constant idolatry skipping breakfast alongside pear-heavy waveforms, quilted observatory bucket scopes as they dwell on operating tables, lactose intolerant 1-800 numbers reviving flare-up.

Encapsulated lariats projected on windscreens divulge something, although no one can discern what luck has been coping with hay mongers welling up to surface latitude *a table* toes beneath and toll booth quills left on Formica gelling.

Chariots lavage occupants partake of outback's lasso. Timothy grass replaces wood paneling with lyre (stitches it) even though oracle summer closes on Sundays every eighth night of famine and parting way, where migraine crease splinters in mesh bevel.

Grass or no, hitched art (kickstart) of the spoken lyre ingrains in us a plenary *vert* made happy under glisten of *am* with recency a plot and stamina foretells of underlines that wheel away from fright pinned to the wing nobody knows can lift from beveled ground.

Wing or is it softshoe, shinbone, contamination? Shy lockets choke the trilling bird, upend (console) a workbench, skinflap of wrench and delta clay pigeon mortuary. All clouds in crosshairs come down sworn into the life where *child* cannot be ordinary.

Bench press ordinal data previously seen through crosshairs genders missed in word, deed, *bonne chance* overtures, loud to midrange (mirage) drilling the wild or airy patch of swoon shirting the chore to spring a soul wrenched from these intervals.

Homo erectus impingement graphs this mollusked marine quarter trans-mogrifying the heaven-toward recall, dermasphere gen-X curfew. Inter-veil, vile, vilify— all these soap opera hopeful arias along hacked Venezuelan fair trade karmas traded up for cash.

Soap-optic activists karm their way to lavish ash made curlicued by vile rinds graphically tithed in red dermography gone ping when lingering calligraphy marked the inflection, where a tonsure might have been, aligning papal quips into milktoast rearrangements.

Blackout radicchio, *la palabra*. Oxen-tick praxis fits warm fey stews. Inlet signs, laterals bitterly print-fed cartridge as intent's king-sized macramé, parked insexed hemp staved off as sable minetrope rips chaperone brusqueness, coastal as quince.

Axes vaulted prime few signatories past the lateral heart chapeaux, unless quintets show bitter staves grammatical with mimesis scalded from the faculty of touch poised near a park where twaddle's omen's ripe for parsing toward kingfishers seeming sparse.

~

Faxing palls (pales). Grime reputes allegories. Last battering shark, p-ar-t (II). Puppet scintillation. Plows litters in behaved attics. With street confession halting difficulty of such noise. Beer stark swaddles snowman pipe-lore. A farci board beaming moss.

Gimme a bat, gimme a park, lupine ravine, a quark from manic stash to roster in a loopy vein voiced bitterly amid wax tactics braced to peel across the ficus where havoc has been fessed to and the low grade water clumps après the toss.

To commandeer "at," on a jiminy lark, supinely we gavel the preakness, trash or foster sin a shooting pain hunkered fittingly as squid-jumping jacks in space sealed off for us care maverick tresses dip in and blow by daughters' unbalanced pigtail coordinates.

Sporadic visits to the salt lick unravel dampness while clamping poster shots at tinkerers in bloodlines leaguey as fingerbowls attracted by freehand brush strokes painting rests between the lines a quid apiece where lone stars squirm.

Epidemiology priss, bolt your chickadees to travel and cramp merriment, the chimney toy-makers hoodwink a sheer delight quaffs our foes' tactic sty of freedom *hush*. Saintly nesting fleer crimes trample split-crowns a "scare" as martinis harvest dust.

Rims of spirits brush and sing, the sheer delicatessing of each glass against each other string of lovely work's elastic vested nest with odes and shimmers latched against the makings of a dowager, substantial and with proven scented leas.

Por favor, refusals. This-is-to. Move the rigor mortis backward to portico and beach. In consequential flyfish flung-forward caterwaul, café (rectangular). Road is organic and chronic, curving to deer on side's rearview river. Coerces sedge to rotor, gravity, glade.

Nudge gains along stints valedictory as silt. The cur(v)e views purview cleated as classic laid. These still shots veer toward wall-flits, moving along ersatz lines with to-from stipules formed to last. And gravy hastens styles. Or points slathered vast.

Birthday song from stairwell mishaps. Fervent slaying wordcoo, meals-on-pilaf Vlassic noem. Braille pill cots uncoil foreplay composites, scooting flickerphoto off its blister, pustule greasing spinthrift. Where stayuplate restores placenta.

Continuum, stark first then cooled by water. In the house yet cooled by specious means, as though entrap meant sophistry and roiling in a daybed threaded with these flittering commas, breath (marks) chalked on walks with siding and new plots.

Escalation is cancer-prone alimony— request & denial, sadistic as such, inimical and discretely sore. Throne-footed Hermes set a lien against this coffin posture or in emote infantile fromage-speak: stoic anhingas countermand their dewy meds.

Friends make good pets. Post-haste derogation plasters a vouchsafing with blade-vistas and obfuscatorio prone to wit, and metrics leaning piercely on a finned posterity with blades and tile hooves rinky as a planet plumed in four tweed rains.

Shaken down minaret, complacent studio of starry fugue, corduroy dealt milli-plectic underwise. Suicide indivisible by 0 over 0 over 1 (*esperanza*) = transgendered zone coolant twists "we" fibers of llama-borne O negative protocols punctured by a-s-d-f.

How to distinguish between whist and bone . . . when melody is hard, the teal of it just scam(p)s and lotto peels off afterthought give ground to tomes divided by their stars. Amendments dress our windows, portions parallel to cider's protocoolant sways.

Off selves in grams and earring amethystine calliope: Fargo's legacy, lethal is heat butterflies hustle to convene, miner's weed springs from soundchamber sonnetry. Debunks scoliotic pane and treatise, constitutional motion leeward vocation leaps.

Piercing the line of code for ramshackle constitution leagues from springs invokes commingling and systemic branches turned rendezvous to boot and safe things are meaning to defrag the cornices and wist with ringtones.

Tunic stumbles upon rewind. Is it any wonder famished absolution sings of coppice and crumb? Sycamore stashes its mansion of chlorophyll, genomic soot waif suede ping jerry-rigged for countdown, mordant pewter zipping up its wonder.

Lumber's mentioned in the dented pew where childhood rubbing leads erosion quite asunder, showing that whatever is divisible by four is equally susceptible to being halved like flakes of snow when cleansing is a withered mishmash of a winded stash.

Saw reigns in with wind-combed folly the overflowing wince participant. Sleet is willing to foot garnish, drink candles' expiation each white wine whirlpools to cedar. Any street sheds its lip-reader psychic whose dainty depression lacks a reticence.

Stampede needs perspire white wine. Cedar chestnuts sleet sideways to side with dappled press of sleeves as the reticent undress. Psyche likes a breezeway, sages staid in mild participation looking out at garnishes purported to be garish.

Mantra. Steeped in. Prius. Requires sight. Finery. Port pressure bunts peat moss hideaway. Scalped game-set-match euphonic duress cops hypnotic bids. Sheepskin sibilant hairstyle glues bands to the wild titillation of enzymes, parishes.

Euphony stipples fine young sense of night. Asculpt with range, the scalp retrieves symphonic referenda for love-fifteen with dispatch into the biding time worn creases to indulge the eyes. Rich seams finagle pathways that accede to knots of net.

Osmotic dimples, orthogonal (crest of leaves or fire) however snug acquiesce pulp where shapeless coves, note's topography has no quip absorbed no leaky petal or brig gripped by skirmish, the hilt of sea, the tip.

Diacritical brocade makes creeping over floor a worthy tryst with sorbitol and leaves brigandily dropped close in to the tip-toe netherware of future dapper look aligned sarcophagi p/laced in and out of scrimshaw bettering the host.

Instant as schematic d-r-i-f-t. Inimitable as rushed repairs, the prune rots but for its wrinkled divestment, lopsided rosary piano jig, kindergarten astutely swears its Crayola catacomb crazed fin wrapper, a burnt umber rickshaw wheel.

One part after another breaks, is splinted to promote free fin through water a cappella, kinder tentatively comb the rinks for slivers of ice while Ian Anderson's the sole rhythmic lumber crayon being the reins not far from vestments on the edge of being razed.

On-star rafter brother stakes his hinted moment, din-blue. Farther from umbrella tinder dent your given bromine pinks pour into styles widely. Inconsistent slumber pales (harrowed) seeing pains shot-hard synapses absolved ray by ray.

Where am? Who are? Is what umbrella pounced ashelving triune lalala ray banned by gauche arrow stung into the napstalk integer momentum dining careful Roth he plants indentations a test the non-walk-on anymore steps one at a time.

Transmission might ask, lap at banks, static on the lean muscle of a grenade. Tributaries soak up their mass to reignite a courtesy. Semaphores invoke their cytoplasmic echo. At best, waltz props up its dead, trembling at its exigency.

Remarkably strewn vises cling to linger near ignition curt in frenzy. Spotted awl spawns pointillist injections only pin deep. Read-only is ready to wear no-fault leisure stalls while classic is laid to pass for anchor when the mission oak stays its keen musk over years.

Demarcate feuds, how price is flung few and far. The meow coffin blurts its tiny host infection. Find your kibbutz, flinch. Write-only earthquake and consider how magic prays for grey fruit canticles thundering July's folkish spleen, how it's spun.

Alignment's a property of forestation. Blunt seed storms ripen sun to grey scale, in which keening of folk runes offers yearning in a field whose infection's flinch has outsized magic near repeated run time error quaking thunder's spleen.

In time with fir and what splices gulf hastens wind's cogent appraisal an ordeal of cures, to which one proffers vinyl and high-gloss ditch for cinched ultra-metallic rattle, the *fait accompli* water-is-denser-than periphery or applause.

One expatiates on the simplest siege, the lure of talk brocades even a ditch with proffered battle. Arms are everywhere, and insufficiently *around,* such that peripheral separation thins the gloss on theory better than facts pried loose from fate.

If expedition craves the prurient speech, "sold" ends too soon. If the furor over enclave pitches flak jacket Amazon into sunrise land-locked spewing itch arousal under its breath as breast. Where Broca's area is excised, moles of starlight kneel.

Spun ilk of seaside lackadaisical Confiteor brims any hocked ridge of I-thou to pews attracting untracked daylight very morning in its pixels seashorn otherwise impene-tacit autoclave removal of the fun along *pied a terre* as raspy as away pointing to loons.

Gun is shrill prescience packing them in genesis, drawbridges stocked boasting huge rhizomes trembling in shack's concerto well-worn shifts lounge-scape of impunity as the autoerotic floorshow do-you-approv*es stand auch geschrieben* a little, no?

Ridged acorn top show low concerto stage right lock stock and host hill poised poison aiming for *poisson* while other species hold still (fear's a lock) thus flocking to non-glow are drones about to go off half-cocked also prepared to hit the floor (even the score).

Missive to aspirate the oak-elm-spruce-birch residential plight. Hock the frost from its pane are-you-dead-inside drawer closing what can be connected to protected scrubs fairly zoned devout even if drops from coming soon an impaled session for the hazzan.

Scrubs fit many vows, even in raw loss. What can be irksome may also fit the sieve's reliable encomium. What is restraint if not the crops resisting airlight? One field or two? The straightedge inside Platonic spear grows increasingly dependent on an outer voice.

And the recuperated masses of telephony to whom Liza goes stapling a forget-me-yes the latitude and wired on-brimming of that impermanent sickness. Pom frites and nausea, parka hood in the scrunching gray of medulla dullness into / out of.

Eyes *yes* their way to permanence in dulcet ways, brimming with eventuality the wired pathos, hooded with restraint mistaken for despair the color super-imposed upon beginning, middle, t/end/erness forestalling envy's masking various robust phonemes.

Chiffon whistles toward apathy in flamboyant séances where written residence clutches bedtime rituals a marathon logic stood up without complaint. My precocious flare up of forestalled complaints, obstetrics of prologue, presage, ordinal and vicarious (sheer).

Planted limbs reflect the prior jeers (curtained calligraphy) in tandem with confinement double-clicked in logarithmic jitters anti-pliant and pre-carousel as if the timing could not be more prone to a presumed sagacity with vicious peerage storming forts.

Licking whose wounds "draconian indictment" speed limit's deadline cedes the key. Go parallels and hit-and-run flatulence. On the border a wildfire probes the unraveling how-do-you-mean. Exhumed naguals inflect sphere's contrition.

Equality amounts to parcels of *how* instead of cylinders afire, *n'est-ce pas?* Or are you robed keystone Copernicus, flat-out wound up, meaning inner sphere's carnauba waxing 40 or so hits' hyped linkage to the music of Ravel, ones nemesis at metronomic speeds.

Si, si, si. The phoenix brokers its mane scowl-breed hindrance. Who bleeps out polished bifocals and safehouse cat-mongering in/the/interest/of/cartel's relaxing the *sine qua non* defamatory watch list sales distortion pedal on loan to space.

Gratitude deflects injurious winter thought residing alongside scrap heap bundles focal to the catastrophic indraw of habitual stall points under lassie-come-home fall guy losing interest, while sequentially being steamed down off the shelf of koans.

Incalculable rejoinder. To wit, anon. Lastly, come home. And in us, nothing. Surgically borrowed. The ambrosia prints its Daedelus metaphor-perfect tropical depressions. Act now for a low, low, low squandering. Principality prods the anecdote. Lease fame.

Posture makes unrounded. Should(er)s relapse into the concrete where first found. Rinsed wings made whole lead home (tropes romp to spring). One motto: Join before rejoining. Meta-notional prestige encompasses before it lasts. Over to you . . .

Accosts brickhouse, yes, human filling station of a portion, or life. *Ta-da*: now you don't believe what's ever been promised, a rook on deck. Tugging the "enter because it will make you free" from spam's domicile where garment gains the weight of blinking.

Pancreatic robbery. There she was again, with whiter hair, in Safeway. One wrote "threat" rather than "treat" about a reading on poetics. Blink. Standard operating proxy spins one premise after a missing style. Who is it performs the heavy lifting?

Confection: (all-fours) anuric moon trifle. Less is more, but minus the vans deferens. Gymnasium dazes to a rain check. Better half down aisle 9. Preachy feeding ad-text plink-O "stop" no-go, but then . . . Militia's preoccupation, triceps erupting.

Plink's notary publicity's about to kink the lawn. Riff of moon supplant the dings in feathering the watch(ful) eyestrain. Stealth for hire. Wealth for lyre. What's in us? Cliffs and mountain hens. The lack of daze is stifling, while the tumors are of course engaged.

Sink is entirely full-on. Proposal to trinket sauna. Strife is ample, dead-center truancy revamping its adept-angel (angles?) risk, stamped and backdated to the pernicious 'caravan' dubbed as: to those in a position of grandeur, restful, single.

Isthmus tromps all over ontological downdraw, and why not? As if a poseur were to fracture the cage. Rage stultifies an otherwise hose-down of rest that singles out the sample touted as ample pragMEsis. Are you cramped among tomes? Don't ask.

Fringed fisticuffs launder their torrential schematic. Scores of them, alone on page 2. What percentile does the hora undress to neck? Pot-shot cramming coincides with foraging, the pampered and study-famished "hi."

Pinched verve sacks rustic stuff, guns up implanted schematography that turns out to be just pampas grass, and blackguards sneeze throughout the room yield of stuffed ballot box, a way through for the percentiles one repeatedly misses by a digit or potash.

Morning glories swerve trigger-happy dazzled & loaded .45 arriviste burnout is scooping three-awned seed heads, florets a-bristle and comatose. Soon a field votes out clusters of the four-leaf extrasensory adrenal dam flourishing versus acronym FLOX in transit.

Bounty blocks the sadness. Florets indulge even those who plan to come in last. Apostrophes go a long way toward nourishing the runners-up while they recoup specifics of their reflex backward float. Some third party slavery costumed to resemble free voice.

Thimble: tri-fortress of thumbs. Back to the winter easel wipeboard, off-the-block. Past. The double quotation. Alternatively, self-injury. Locker room of one mild germ's interlocution. Dura matter, mansion grey. Pastry-shaped as the scar on your verb.

Placation's not vacation. Trim / slum / beat / white. The lockstep boards up jury's slump block juncture twice blocked by the bled slow weave of verbiage. Vast wild lumber takes us where? If self is bounty, just think of what these twinned renditions might imbue.

All too often (a sense of irradiated amounts). What's partitioned there?
Dumping either synth-e-tic bodega by bulleted lists or some slim weed
unlabeled Gemini along coal tutelary trails where green lightning fixtures
(fixate) turbines to the florid Libra.

Binary unction dwells amid *belles letters*. And why not? Libelous charges
prompt word bullets half imagined by one versus two. Coal energy may limn
some gentle line across the plain page left green wood to fix upon the flora
various uninterrupted acts of fawning.

Accent representation is swanky shelter. Whoever it inundates: *circumflex* =
caret vs. *cedille* = *comma*. (Synerg)(n-thesis) & quinces— aplomb as face time
gasps (shun-ista) pro bono pulp 6:30 PM taps angel's *should* in campfire TB
relaying its Vonnegut welt.

Bulbous ixnay angles sashay to the boundary plummetless in ordinal ways
through cabaret-style torsion fired to manufict the dizzy lines of codicil where
a binomial scent of weltanschauung gives back nerve-Anna to her peers, her
sheltering kin.

Curtain's fandago wrangles a bindery, call to defibrillation. Meta-data skins,
fornicating odd/even whales, the trampled consortium: good girl, bad girl. She
is heroine, housed in a Jill-come-lately sash wizened by observatory's ditch 'n
drag, subluxated to waste.

How fast heart skin hears, when tramping about the ragweed. *Luxe* conforms
in general to ash, to waste, to good girl bad heroics, consorting with(in) nicks of
time and temperature [all fibers wrap whales] wizening qua servant leader
bracken ditched.

Outtake has fastened us to brim and tooth, scalpel is orating in Betadine.
Expounds the zipper-like, gaping monastery's plug & play vault spent on
spouts (see fallen alliterated kettles, antiquities of the controlled Welsh Farm
fables apprenticing seeds).

Clean, clear brown's impounded recollection holds in frame the view of eighty-
six eighty-six address, the opposite of monastic pouts, contraption, far away as
water, inferentially a contretemps reed-thin though laced controllably with X
and double thus in view of us.

Knot the thunder only if *they* want to withhold three hundred or more pounds of diameter. P.O. box scarecrow hours on the up-and-at 'em, waning stature checking into the motel on Rt. 6 (walks the wire of raffle or blood test) confederate y & z-strains, coyote-cute.

Mute verses moot versus pluck and at-it-yewed alongstruck cloture *arrive* a bit prema- (pass the brulè) the angles that wire me a folk dance, maturation's fancier than looking at you askance, the care's in escrow blink on blink off with fed rate strained to boot.

Deliberately skittering into soot, pinafore spiffs its underpond enough. Boojum revives valley-esque and soffits tear from derby arches prepping their starsearch mandibles for crucible counters begging for — shutter-step— flee— skip— leukemic free-for-all.

Vivisection parks predisposition nearer roadway than the curb. One searches before lurching toward (im)prompt(u) from the front row leeway fleeing point five pond(er)ing assumptive plaudits envisaged spiffed enough to escalate toward transom's g(l)ut.

Trepidation's Izod rain of meter-tunic quartered stomach. To re-avenue (avail?) itself breathes stoplight. Where improv(is)–sat ion al *stage left* remits its slain bow-corpses anonym's challenger is elegiac, dull. Hard foam dresses harming his euphonic rib.

Anklets torque the elegiac prose, sated with mitts where metrics ought to have felled ripeness, roaming charges, belles-letric euphoria. The blues lack rhythm, but the spires are teak. Oh Romeo, deliver trespass under glass and glide stage autoharp toward me.

Practicum or protrusion is genre, is vignette, is *raison* (risen). Allow it to come through pure loops of synesthesia, minutes used in the bathroom until crooning stacks your fifty pallets of timothy fume and privation. One eats salmon with a spoon as violins do.

Crimpy say-so rips through genteel harvests synthesizing twill and keepsake. Focused on mundane, lined paper for the wayward notes, the tacked-on process toward dour etchings. Loops for b-fast, *raison d'etre* still light fast, herbal roughage on the rise.

Skimp on cheating leaves from their cradles. Infantilizing willing to borrow —
no more Ns to spare kid, so don't enter here the votes they are poisoned, not
kettle-cooked like promise, fork of incline. Saber cereals rattle the toy, the
reinforced metal of opposites.

Tin toy forced posed cauterist entrepreneurish look-alike fan tilly row row
robust rattle's radical one-shot *vote aqui* confection tipping up north heat leaves
unread tea from unimposing numbers young folk differ among selves their
mettle and their poses.

Cinderblock titter swami circumlocution simmer to the skin the waistband's
saddled upstart elastic activational goodness ease faked for minstrel
condemning slumbered frappe stokes the january lease where nodule says Do
not pass go.

Circumspect, a synonym, she asked to band the stitch with saddle good to shaft
indemnity by nod to wit the go-light's energizing yes to paint and stretch and
rap stitch via Walla Walla understruts with active feed line don't touch lumber
once.

Miffed doesn't begin, pounds everyone into knitting. The vocational paddle
rewinds resounds. Infirmary sod. Pistol-whips, *thank you for* venerable shame
of whittled canopy. Ejected overseas *tag* you're-dead, everybody frets,
severing next of kin.

~

Kit closure, vox populi, wind instruments. She played bassoon, as stilted ones
must do, averting thereby shame same flag and head-lips-feet set-point,
severely kindled if one must, and rust inherently blips spates of veneration
titillating though the addled be.

Kittens dipped in populace or pony ride heat index & estrogen bad grade
embellishing. He sweated his semen in the dark of operating room reserved
seating, brass section out of decibel grain alcohol exit-lane, copper nerve is lent,
leaning, framing *is* in *was*.

Preowned hectare radishes turn lexical, and there is room for service of the
brass, rain stalling alcohol beside the copper pans that gleam as ductile jewelry.
Prognoses lend themselves to nerve crèches on account of mornings with sweet
carapaces.

Monies change hands as hexameter shifts to lounge out the wikipedia windfall. Arrange narcotically the gowns used to cook 24kt from contextual substrate. Get the I out of yourself so it will be vindictive, rambunctious into the 11th hour.

Narco-vanity rambuncts the ninth month whether anyone looks wickedly or numbly at the sun. The stilted level carats brink change the hex placed to right where it belingers and the limelight of cash embedded in the text remains continually sub-par.

Sontang stiffs the essay's potable theorem. Come bearing child or drink the flash of quotidian Oz. Finesse the arbiter into coincident cash 'n carry edges, if insight deems it sufficiently stifled to fetch the specification 8.5 inches deep with quarry.

Posture the noble auspices and Pisces if amenable. The incident's appalling for an inkling and then lashes in high numbers stiffen the frail thumbprint of a retching noise. Drinking the earth informally will venerate its streams. Sufficiency means fortune, seems.

Yonder yard line, rejoicing venial Chernobyl, and the unfriendly signatory packs it in. Dry-heaving *uh-huh* would not worry so much about concessions of identity, ribonucleic scallion epoxy stutters loose from Euclid, finding an infuriation to get sore by, poor.

Roaring Fork displays a habitat the mood ring scuffed and concentrically furred by store and taught to fear Venetian slips of light-through dentifrice as friends sport signs and act out poxic stunts as lucid as a culp and wringing stoic censure as the lien's left hanging.

Victual not volume as doled into apocryphal Naya of bilification w-o-r-n around its spasm crease baffled from walk-in closet eucalyptol incentive not clinically proven while placard grunts the blackjack table bruises easily over levitated corridors of noon.

Trim time on task crafts standards against chalkboard yielding trounce across ounces in tents, their recency non-primal, roving 'round each round known patch. The laugh about her white hair tangled against a thin historic mist bereaved (the once thatched quest).

She euthanized the weedpoint in Borneo south of the Suez byways flume hitched to chickee hut smoke sleepover bent navigating the skinned peach of earth its fleshy pantheon saccadic principle silver-groved eye massaging dew point at its phalange.

Lexicography points to cheeky bitmaps in the navigable unitext. I dream of how you prince toward silver lineage. That would be now, when crowds, skinny eyed, impose quiescence merging with neglect astride the (m)eager solo acts (protracted).

You, who poses, may give up this honor and come to a concentricity out of desperate someone green to the concert, no more horses left, babe to suffer lowghost improvement you're doing (how you always do) clandestine as its marrowless face.

Hoarfrost simmers in the mind of arrow's plot posthumously in a sleek print to the right of the driveway trickling as if substance might be imputed from a concert. Whose oboe is it? The repairs included reed-only, all in one shrill clobber.

"The book of Gwenivere needs a drink" sipping sounds as t-t-t-t (with no h) (nothing in h) streaks to viscosity and why, if one is bearish as allegory, frigate hunches down balled up under cunning (cut) & lingual eddy of cocktail carousels. Bloodiness neatens you.

Is fake the avarice one counted? Blastoff carnivals trim nature from a natural re(s)po(n)se. Is there a proctor in the residence? Bear markets bare the sologram all wedged into a lingua freak show eddying around the rink of pressure's reassuring spark.

No one in their right costumes, unaccounted for, allow the spear to wander the archer's quiver. Stem is oily and coming up with real estate or stain's burlesque future after diet the poem exerts. A level of feroc- (felicitous) preakness (*speak*) fat of the helium utopia.

Teaked (tweaked) to the titular Endymion, one rapcalls further south, tailing through archways and being wholly stemmed. Party charms invoke subtraxis shake roof dowries until prim felicity seeks only spokes (when spoken two-timed) altogether cellular.

Tête-à-tête on Mount Latmos where antipathy is curvaceous, pick-pocketed from the cupola where tranquil ken (eyes)—whose?—repelled seventy kisses, protean alimony & diasporas beams quilting northeast flocking to refinement on the dialed pall of stone.

Leviticus dusted for prints leaves little doubt of what is missing from the tent of acrimony severing the wince from nature and blackmailing sippers of latte into pocketing the story following the story rumored to be the sole story, kisses or brushfire notwithstanding.

Affections wheeze a channel-click stammering *thou* and *shall* disturbed zooming into Chappaquiddick, the insatiable fabulist: autumn festival stirrer and frothing frigate scantly heralded biserial hazard lane. Hop to it, wish this upon fuss, rush in. Demand it.

Second commingling solves thousands of zooms that cut to the quick to find a found lane drawn in thirds. Distributorship seems only yesterday's song. Broth bears Alice's brusqueness. Pass it on. The mandarin exclusion trembles with fistula revealed.

Stall door barges into lop-eared odyssey, confounds the gear sneezing agitates enigma's road crew off-ramp teacup— nausea impresses, retrofits algebraic mast tournaments, years, all objects abscessed (smile) where jars gather rubble, breathe.

Tactics mean the world is drying. Years take back the paltry fall of newsprint, the parking lot where woman as robot left her meal, prompting a departure of all others from the tiny space as though stubble were a launching pad, found charted, and gears finely worked.

Neither lap nor Julia's suspicion uproots the fabricated laxative of thirst. Betrothed as one is to Proteus, due for neverland, categories rappel down the outfield's only wall. Strike three names the intimate in saddle-stitched unshaven strep throat apprehension.

The set pulse leaves us cold from all that failure to cry. Siren baskets empty themselves and neighbors, purported to have shared the field, the wall, blame prehensile possibility, until the spikes enter the wood of definite particulates (still pulse).

Anemic flurries lend sound into-these-gaps-with-caution, deer's tongue stews whitely among the faint of being, and scrolls *la meme* township's fallow rack where twilight attains its body, thesaurus of night's fecund silver rakes its reef awake.

Aloe s/oftening the skin. Conditioning aught to form primary numb(erstwhile) c/raft there(by) depletes an enormous storehouse (Stockhausen) in the act of following the few with attention, post-scurry qua liver spots delineating twilight's free twills.

Antiquated bin of heart's twice-wrapped furl. Innerscript is width the score-is(gorge)ous as ventricle, logarithm dissecting orange slices on pint glass emblems of slippage, sight lined to the hilt rabbinical wallop, swift uppercut g'mornin after dark has bitten.

Leave the litre near the bin. *Turn off the set.* Core gorges feed the heart to rhythms in a mood of sector lint. Blancmange served au gratin yields a string of wisdom, or a vast warm sky finned through by youthful curiosity, cut with ratcheted ark markings just lit.

Sharpener vatic as the point-click-drag (disposed of) yoga ligament. Thumping brood of crash-apportioned child. Appetizer fields a ping of sincerity, icons leap at the tragic voweling of pure noise. Pop-up recants a million tea lights.

Lump together rash and you get wrinkled dashboards, conical dreams, rim-shot cavities. Posture toward the sacraments and you get consonants that cantors fling. The tea runs mist across the yard, proportioned so the point is breath, not noise, not rude. Not cash.

Stumped and forgotten, how the louvre of odometer and mileage consecrates fealty open-ended stairs equipped in the amen of demotion, role as simple son via ravines' equating link of kissing & egg hunts condensed to afikomen.

Miles to twirl before dense kissing's quasi stair light in the full consecutive of morning shaped by vines' links and the looking. Draft integrity mourns instructive sadness for the simple to be right in this museum of promotion. Vast and shouldered and arriving.

Even differentials invite the miner's lettuce into escalation, penny to the well-pleat. Indignant fire thinks "red vinca" as it flags across latticework, micron tougher than vent respires its fool's errand in crass hydrolytic colonies, cedar staves and sister cities.

Colonial cedar blanks out use despite the escalation of pleated digs. Where lagging growth emits a fire, one thinks too roughly near the balm and random rasps from fields where penny wisdom flourishes as mined resolution jitters its way through.

Shapeless mittens parry barrels, shafts appearing 'round the stained counterfeit railroad. Collect calls sack the community chested coriander-scented firework, fluidics of such a price and oddity that inquisition faints beneath the swaying troupe.

Rehearsals for depth perception, the wool piece, the sack cloth vested in work marker down library copies of the lubricants that sway from trope to tropics heaving their way to the grain from sod when rice is all that nests in sound.

For which parade, mother-bird's junkie itch. The thinnest of metal planes, a coin-chewing tin man as omniscient (self-proclaimed) fading forest doomsday where fairies lose their grapheme seaweeds, thrive on day-old crepes pickled in chorus.

~

Lane change, vetted rest stops, close quarters fed into the dry machine shop strike one thin line radicals (free) chase water back to source (perfect) as if memory were daylight. One panders to prophetic climax when metallic gold coast fritters west.

Prefigures jams and U-boat wrong turns — Jack, Jack, could eat nothing, his head so full of gum tree sap and scansion hash mark *going down dear* SOS cramped, upload. The plow a north one must review, wire tap dance its anklets against acedia.

Plumlets grace the dark in kind, mementos practice being bringing back the impulse on first base. *Are you fair?* A gimlet's worth of boring offers incisive views of down home blockades like mother used to makeshift as a tap game sparring anklet against flow.

Impacted with nightwatch a garden likewise bobbles the pitch and inflames its dare: the umpteenth court conquered by maps. Arthur resuscitates the maiden with olives and oxygen, gloves wet, a Polaroid's weather. As if eroding from mirage (starving it).

Watch that photograph for subtle changes, mirage is an acquaintance of sotto magic, the teeny aptitude for foraging recuses selves we didn't know we had, including Rodman on the court (recall?) androgyny's a mere forecast forestalling maiden voyages the allure.

Sexless confidence of the daemon, skin-rip. Vitiates the torpor, *la hermana* ditto. Stance. Hot topic in Monmouth calibrates a drill, funneling balls down 3rd, be sick— pronto. Priceclub examines (hacks into) every Transamerican myth delaying launch.

Haunches repay hunches in full. The stench of erasure faults lemony salvation, its stature and linguistic gnosis. Calibration is the act of leaving out the blips. *Confiteor deo omnipotenti:* Do not bother taking back. Removal's hyperbolic. Lunch trumps launch.

Outskirts the noxious fang-strike of Brady kiss, benched indefinitely among khaki & twill. Agnostically let-go. Blindsided middle of night shedding its viceroy evangelical aroma et lux perpetua es (is) (light) (and) (forever) revamped. Fed to a clause, tramp as mirror.

Try age, press gnostic, press pastiche. Low-cost singularity makes raves with rivulets (the will to forget) *c'est ca.* And sides are often blind. Remember them, the quicksand of skipping rope to gravity . . . one has not played. The time was: This hand. This lift.

Going stag, storms of backgammon and beach (ratted out). *Ah* is the diagnosed sturdy magic, recall a shrine's immaterial aches what equus tabulates & overfills zoology with. Quintets assert loudly to a monorail. Byzantine isotopes distend a rhythm's hearth.

Brat force lacks tithing. A glottal word is worth the busywork it's smitten with. Zoology convenes the sharp and shapeless fans of mono sitting bedside the television's IV raging ostensibly across counters about aches and pandering.

~

Agrarian hinterland. Take five. Hedgerows drag into probable cause the lecherous stalks. Violet paramours double as sinkholes to the tinny furtive conch. A strewn ellipse entangles its raven with blue jay, with zero. Take π, for instance, the price tag.

Five sentences sink in. The couch is strewn with ragged tin and blue. Probable warbles make her voice in jest. One misses the day when mezzo sop turns dizzy high then goes low. Although the warmth of that exceeds the human status paragram.

Glam vindicates the mink imperative, declares it sin, tantamount to quart-sized mime type, fetal divide. Lounge prunes its clockwork for soprano run-through, flies das boot hermetically this furniture of pulse intensively in a paradigm's vendetta.

Implacable enemy centers the heart, locked into work files never tantric (trick sized) plaint divisible by three unless the ounces glued to pulse seal war glyphs into psyches prana filled and clued, or not a place to sit beside tensile hastenings, dogmatic.

Mana is elevation ready for fool's dough kneading its treatable metabolism, a hand-me-down saint. *Is that your card?* Chimeric flounces out of its coffer, shipwreck stunt binds mind to the encephalo(what) mothertongue blast ingesting marketplace chatter.

Flatbed rucksack embellishing formats, reform off-hours wrecked in the stun gun mind waves tongue smart and gestating some wise treason toward the need of saintliness (look at the graph, look at the sun shield) quietly regard the raft.

Towing the delta flaps-up over indigent crosses, voluble powwows take on bilge. Pin-up graves sung tart among a fan base diuretic. Its heiress spills a prettiness biting down on third world aether (thesis) recycles debt-affected domes for the straggling few traces.

In lieu of a domestic flap, the cycle was blimped into spastic atmosphere as if to tamp down the diurnal lark made grave, pinned to dross and lithe divergence tapped out of the trove of stung mass (sung Mass) based on heirloomed repellent for the shark out front.

Pang or Great White. Whose heterogeneous voice skips through plutonium pores drilling shores into antecedent heap, the bodies aggregated, caving thrones plugged, panting as the baroque lower jaw amends one proximity of spray, one halting hello, or halo.

Suppress, remand, excuse. Those enlisted bundle the tones of gluten where rills might stand to plumb the deep executive cave disguised as ladder constantly amending a foreshadowed tense. The law ensues and comes to outcast.

In the mirrored earth, repopulated by a retina, howls quaint bounty shivers revealed dumbly when festooning the skin moves on its own recognizance, fending off triple plays and recounts. Ill laws are like the sores of a crowd on volcanic plateaus.

Pratfallen isotopic grovels give fender light swift lip, borrowed from cognizant settlers made to pitch their flaws hermetically sore from rowdy kin who lay aside differences and find new dumbbells to populate the empty cells our anxiety would fill. (His, hers)

Must have the vale (evinced) how they perambulate hunts purchasing their Louisiana *bless you thanks* tactic shreds hapless garage band dowdy currents in line with watershed give-back and nautilus paper boats near lithium's hopscotch morgue.

Breath is its own advocate. One hears the lisp of treelight in the spheres on grows among. And letdown beams its butterfly taupe surely as the lineage pays homage to pronunciation's Catskills overdrawn and rendered via eye-hand memory coordination.

Ball descends through gnat's eye, vaulted urge, watchful demagogue, hearings round table one traipses across, riverdance the *la-la-la* head up *la-la-la* wing down ameliorate pinnacle of Proustian inches (pop-up blocked) synaptically pointing its shrill fatwa.

Swann's glowing repartee or not, the sun slits through imaginary windows, *music for use* available to the untrained eye, and lockstep revelation of a fastened knowledge of the mother's movement upward through the spiral nicknamed home's own sin of mind.

Splashing iniquity's corsage so revolves a chakra in the interim. Take a moon, frozen in its valent swivel, holly red, whatever insole, chelsea house, villa, landslide, or porch cigar-smoke embryos sucked from gravel cuffs, surname teased, the tiff of ulcer invoked.

Clear first. Refract spun live one, roses are not carnate spores. The slipping land mass orchids its way into psychometric cufflinks until ulcerous recall provokes the tantrum term from limits tucked in breadbox left on first. The syrup clip reminds of clutter's clash.

Crater in every fold of tongue. Roses are black as veins, freight whistles, breath, total abdication, laced with chalk silent ringing once over, soon over here. East, whose east, is kept out of view. Limits dye indelibly, saying who is not weak, who goes toward it.

Quiet is the empty place, also the full, where risen flowers include young thistle, and the rests defining measures hinge the rooms with calm connected breathing timed by virtue of felt talk when language equals pulse defined as compass points and magnets.

Waist-high soiree of fire, thrown out at first. Bunted willow (thunderhead) prods the cur. May: drowsing horizon cries foul, the hard arpeggio stalks frosting over weeded hue. Triple myriad of somnolence, indoor lisp of tamarind, astrophysical and stygian as sight.

Glass brick see no clear arpeggio. It hurts to know skin blue. If somnolence, then tapping sound from indoors where slight rowing shifts the arms and then a horizontal occurs to headlines. The brunt of any calling is its a priori genus. Now the hour just fades to you.

Sun rattles its sopping footprint among the octane greeting: *dear constantine* it's difficult to have skin defoliate a brogue, feign its accent, affix your emergency exit to the head of the Charles, open-armed, tweaked by locusts, typhoons canvassing ruby sepulchers.

Learning colors in a brogue enlivens non-emergency's sweet vastness via custom when syllables sprawl into vowels following their little fence print styles of teething and the wind matches the yard with tulips and with clothesline dancing bodiless under the sky.

To starboard, obstreperous impediment of the dialectical: expanding into rainbow-mustached waves, *when in Rome* parts its bloom, yellow & pungent Inca ruins the bassinet of centuries, acclimated, dripping hooked pansies, 80-watt flannel speartips.

Rock and toward, forthcoming lipstick and the motion carried, lines made bow stretch longing leeward also foot markings of lexicograffiti unguent and show shaven so runs of few press synthesis osmote their riptide to the lotion shore, the priestly place, the dome.

The derelict spray, proof is rouge, cosmetic as dream, rough-meet, help none. Fines they score unto, herewith, shall bring a *forget-me-forward* astrolabe attached to plaque matched by blade, cicadas and blue agave, skydiver salves to emptiness and altar.

Reams of one include with breast, and there are ivy things. Pronounced young laboratory animals, sung speed of the cicada blue, to wit rest stop and tines the pray for us commencement offers yet largesse all drama winter. Keep the sake in part alive.

To cheat the intestinal and phallic herd, agrestic vurt, league of unplugged simulacrum habitat trail a pr(ism) of catgut, graphite year scalds orthodoxy, braying, waltzing at antidotes, such coolant of grass, a juice of tassels, gray apartment: vow or cumulus.

Priapus dredges little music from the tithing, and Ray-Bans deflect skylight. One shops for cool-decking to resist scalding that would spoil the wheat grass, thus mute thinking quality, despite a nest of cumulus cloud feathering with scant evidence of moisture.

Dillydallying launch in ten, or sacked in five, claw or front-loaded life, banned chess caucus, its checkered rods, cones, pressure differentials loyal to the fasting cornea, necrotic kidney inn, respite for a whittled pill (lightning) in soft-shelled Cassandra.

How she wastes her daylight one-at-a-time protrudes in front of sorry eyes affixed to how she spins the damages stage right into a curtain stained with royal habit, another interim dimension of the odd lot trades that hinder mint from seeming in condition, arriving fast.

Ledge is Prilosec, parenthetical, hype O-knight to her sweat-clothed "as if this" — a kiss is eyed, adumbrates pillow fight, the staid involution. Prophesizes never to be swan, swapped out for garage sale 'o fire, relativity's (sic) quiet claptrap shut-it pseudonym.

Rapt in sequitur of winter, she I he we grant something to low lace and the prophet (may she join us) willows how in white the parents knight a very to privilege. Is town amendable? And are the shut lids also quaking just a little? Fire is kin to sense of sight.

Autodidact snows a gray network, polarized flake of non-anything, imperializes the prorated lance (he-to-a-she advises, adapts, squirrels out prima nocta for thrill ride vermillion) proudly round, but irascible, think another mineral-hard flame as scabbard.

Is the temper only thin when white? And fragile, pale, gray snow line almost wintrified to make the glass matte where a mineral lace changes the view. At night the ration of divisible mistakes goes thin to film and water matches vice. The tender prayer is ice.

Blizzard is masonic, thrifty with its clouded sconce. Footage of blank yard 8mm icecap where emperors wear grizzly furs case the joint flowering lid super-imposed star stripe additive a mousetrap bucking coin toss ratios: red 40 caking on Achilles' palatial glare.

Gallery grist means mill town's not a safe. Yet footage harbors hope beneath its sconce collectively intuited as though rain were on the thresh- and pillars of communal piety were off duty this long while, trapped on 40 acres being tossed atop a fleeting overhang.

Where portraiture flutters? Fabric nation for a fast-drawn proctor, many silks scarfing up the bow. If maimed lamb makes it to the ark in time, tapered leg— port of call steroidal lesson plan in sunset-gunshot, cup of chaff, meal to acreage's tightly coiled wheat.

Vestments sometimes taut will usually shine. Row, row, rhyme your reason, lamb cake is Iscariot because the roids are pinching sets off half-lives eel-like along the acres of untidy wealth, despite presumption of the stealth positioned heavy on the heat pump.

Plink, punt the grail, collar-nouvelle. Skip, boon, start the rigged spark. Season, scam heretic of homerun sting, plundered, met stumped. Trunk peeled, marinara feels fakeness in titanic gobs, crass marina, steam projectile of stake, docile chores.

Armistice jams thought with theorized string. Lumps of projection lumber along in view of cameras obscure as runes. The opus diggity projects a stance, eel shaped Riviera championing clinks and clutter amid raspy thoughts of knobs in lakes with silt.

Chinese red, cinnabar gasses giants sputtering to cherry. Pit sky soaks bicyclists urea and paunch askew. Lenses tilted at the papal asteroid Acme rearing up cord asunder. Wet minion circling roof, glassed-in Leith, lady of the branch-bound grackle.

Watch: the empathy under rooftops passes for viewpoints splayed into an avian effect. As ants, we move together, and each encyclical derivative gives rote rendering a lilt amid the fray, a clue gone nattering, having passed the pewter overclothes of living well.

Vade mecum: blotches the apollonian gray, brief enteritis, symptomatic, blubbering stumbles onto a trail held back fifth grade colored outside uncool call of the call. Built for toughness, gaiety. Bric-a-brac gangly solving its indispensable nature, height-oiled.

This book, this empty, even constantly used emptiness, limbs vector lubrication-lit and railings are not there to lift radical side tests all rough crackling and distended. Lease-purchase lock-steps our bearing to be lore, that in the future calligraphs will show.

Priss chattanook. Concup- crest is eulogescent. Pudd-ump, pudd-ump the aeroverse piston chugs its schooner blurb of nerve-radio-bravado. Move that quickly in a while to scallop the sulfuric deed pricklessly hooped both feet down on the stallvein growhut.

Not to have resided within mores leap yeared, owned intransigence lubriqué as stevedores lay prismic near the chattel having been the chattel to the quicksand levered and foreswayed heavenly hemplined toward a wicklet pretense overcast, mussed crest.

Scud-tested a day less than bilked plentiful hypotaxi(s) in city lisa de mon ravine. Ponds (great lakes) spackle the chapel's frill. Very well, thank you for toking vinery of triumvirate up to ones annex, easterly knee on hyperbole, tousled down.

Taxonometric see-through vinesap lines the rill as nexus bowled across oneiric knee. Whose symmetry's compatible with least-sum-of-ilk. Some nattering's in need of milk toke blasphemous to will the wellside charm to rant-free prose quite unlike Dickens.

Fagin's rags corningstone motor, huck and jive. Solar plexal, the mowed clonidine-licking spree. Trinidad in Tobago, matte black elk, how one gets the horns, free from plinths spoken for / against / printed obeisance: a farm of riddles, fob to cloud, smirks out of it.

Shines forward and back an intense sunshiny riddling loud and mirthful holding pat(tern) whimsical unequal to survival instinctive stature not quite smooth yet not quite wobbling a consecutive prepared rim shot plastered over undertone and thriving in the shade.

Kabul standing in as crawler, stop sign autographed by bullets, corner aces folded high against bridge's lacuna night, riled to half-mast, boardroom bionic slider sphere of toil. Shush of finger to flicked crickets' moby twinge inside satori pert black-eyed peas.

Nigh shoulders lean into right click after oars, later on graffiti's merely spherical, the detention status flickers until candle fall, then wings emerge in thought, the lack of ease, the old and signatory cataract shields ridges from being tactile in full foreground.

Begs an infestation, paddleboat cloves a blight (spectacular) serum, one given on-the-house. Three minds impolite foam their brothel at you, assume a sterile visitor. No-help hooved as one might defend, jerry-rig an excuse or backwater to compliment a scent.

While in line, beam a child to calm him, and the room, after a while, returns from jagged sterile to blue lake, very shiny, for the whole of us to agree upon. The compliment comes from anywhere, with nothing to fend off, summative mind uplifted beyond even the shine.

Sleep terror resides in a mobile Inc. roams if he/she chokes the bathrobe-belted neck bled pregnant with cubes, hunches, clubroom azaleas— multifarious disagreement clones the swarm, swaps its moans, bonuses, om-sick yeast feasting on its petunia mat.

Stasis ought to be magnetic, but it's not. Flame azaleas subdivide attention between warmth and lobbing across nets gargantuan compared with mini-minds of agonists perpetually veiling over joy that must be hypothetical in keeping with the spewing dance.

Uptick the do not enter do nothing but wait, flare ones cheeks like a puffer washed up voice godlike if fire is not invigorated with its fuss or command-ment imperative triad hypnotist to winter theory plods criminally effete sans comeuppance accruing chance.

Odds are, fetes will be remanded to least sum of focus, when the wind, in the wind gives up by being just the stripped down storybook of fire. A Lenten sheaf of withering remarks left on the page is called a letter, pressed some-where, sans luster and sans gods.

Sands! And other sands. Solomon occasion, to roll the die & displace (phrasic shade) croaks— unhand me disband the jet-fumed La Niña. Fumar (to smoke rapidly out of el hábito) scruff (is sage) bustle of salutation, Mingus of modelo cerveza, the shaken ream.

Good everlast. A mild subset of the band empty of note modes, remade sound in which to bask in un-rough fumes, let's call them fragrances. A tool and dye offered to shake loose the ampersand, replace with letter press. Table of random numbers, I confess.

In ones, riddance, subpartition, brittle and nonplussed think thunk codes graves in hunger a village of axes, clinched, found out, stabilizers, wrist samples. Louche as bootlegged superstition semi-confided ink lung bling of colophon and bluster.

What is pain if not perpetually localized? Its left boot status happens to be bled onto the *same page* where we all purport to strive to be. Who bothers with neglect? According to legend, the river sheds its riverbottom way of life in favor of the gray veiled pithy sun.

If a scrum manifold material manifests (man) deadwoods (low) sidereal hipflask and six-shooter, abjuring its open heart operational hazard as if house poor peers in on lavatory carrion birds torching (mothers) givers of fog from horizontal raptures contrails diving in.

Let's all play the depths of strategy into constituent parts and leisure over rapture by the side of the retired moon where frogleaps suture kismet vines and housemouse lavabo clinches the abjured, in-arrears Sumatra flavor that trumps sheet rock flask and chill.

You are not behind the obligatory stride. Prep school resort course spatula reads like a nature trail, Mare Imbrium, costumed canteen scaled down hindways as in belated mountain dross, concurs pin with milkweb compresses lip-coin to a tear, a tee.

Bequeathing sanity to iconographic floss affords a view of better dresses as a form of retort. Nature rails against indignity or likens stipples to a frayed waltz no one's doing anymore. No one's in possession of a mare. Such steep trails mainly warrant lenses.

Beneath it—vanity—blows obvious ( ) into today, garages the rare converg-ence m & m deposits a pretty orbiter trammels its concourse. Of undetermined faith, the I-Caesar so-what-is-there-to-do-about-this deserves a mane. 20/20 exposes the lee of the gallop.

A proxy veto shows up after salad bath. Return of service lends itself to capitulation when in daguerreotype and plaudits rain their smithereens of cope/no cope where on-the-verge deliberation rests like the defense. Are you in mourning yet? Is there a glyph?

Do the 1800s in picayune strain? Would coup *coup* the bipod? Shepherd pointillist carving station into furnace? Finesse the ceiling fixture and sow reproval? Canteen soluble headroom and waive the pint of palliation? Naproxen the mob? Convert it?

iPod trumps bipod trumps guy pad. The point of all this fessing up is that the waves are grief. The waves loom deep. A pint leads to tinged quartz. Do you believe in rain? A fixity be-trinketed by headlights grooming roaming wild-ness? Five or forty new young men?

Housing a playlist imputes the victory to a bushel. See script of corn-maze anagrams structural post-social & gone postal counselors high holy day due to some serious I/O errors, accessorized by Pacifica puns from where juniper flows viciously to Monday.

Why is he so feathery slant low to the wind's impeccable accessories? Or how do holy days preempt the succulent house? Socratic scree contorts a frappe one would have thought was furious. Instead, for now, the brisk Pacific sleighs renorm workings-in-wood.

Scry the loggerhead, punted there out of bounds, not totally unassailable, dispirited patient as midrash Adlerian passage bottom of the fifth Beatrice in pajama-footed corner office sadistic memoir firmware begun with To: exceptionally a pistol will do.

Half tix opens ops for Coptic noir unless reduction stays a sauce and pickled greats are booked in to the potter's wheel in fidgets while the hounds presume to have been blond against the granular mist-revelation of the B-foot joint at bottom a decree.

O fortuna is ecumenical Fabergé a vinegar of abridged lows and two performances of glazed watervein Costco and rope-burn keel are you ready for some Amtrak back to the factious crucible? Capital (el capitán) fatal theta prince skin depleted of vitamin.

Low-flying crux drives a glaze across beheld skin, possibly the onus of experience. On some kind of an even Amtrak one precises forward toward finite depletion, only to await October, when confines of dis-mesh are stalled, and leave away the white.

More twins, they cry, hint blazing out the imperial bay of metal folding chair libelous crucifix lows like a beauty queen on her birthday refilled for free, 30th street high as vault of mayday mayday stargate-1 renews ingot, a mooing gold-on-black latter day trough.

Quill mantra expo-s as if looming shields were doldrums and the color fall-guy stiffed with philanthropy as if taller than god fearing guilt prompts. How does your garden orchestrate the nutrients when rain free flowers their leaning toward white glow.

Smartly seen turning the absorbent stem of paper wall asbestos gears conflated equally broken elm-snow of motel carpet inferior cusp collage your own vegan string section dapper chino border perimeter of Turkish poppies fallen to vice.

Decades of stains make pictographs about to be erased, once snubbed by shifting polity. The fork seams roadways strung to gather laser parkway, at least so anyone might join commiserati in their ringside brokenness popping with platelets yielding voice one prime.

Implication: theatric pap of burrow / beg / borrow. Retracing fubs the sly hilarity. Grifter sues mork 'n mind (rerun) vernacular phasor on stun though parking space is literal, obliged to Pythagorean sandlot royalty sealed with policies and hair o' the dog.

Speak just once to theory-free nit picklets of a neighing boor who rimshots selfish ploys as if and only inference were vascular then phased-in cellular then hair-free clogged impertinent young dog just right for theater but imprecise to guide through fog.

On demand, the horns aim low at the trust, the thrust of newt. Here is Delaunay his catatonic wheel, connection now connected, joke's tower shaved off punchline alongside rectifiable purrs, ticks wedded to curtain of pronoun, possessive, and plural.

Rusted awol cardboard jack, the power to fleck upon dry surface ("land in hand") immerses in verse loudly roaringly and pluralizes as if only the husks of damage were as soft as sudden fleas that occupy the condominia of the unenlightened disowned mines.

Encrusted for selling dialogue, chartreuse outlet, bandied cologne bruiser (new year's) warning lap. Hearse V8 autosexed to the pit pending classified action under mandibular dimple. Latex wing excusa me patched through maximum occupancy in the lead car.

Rehearse is just the stapled start. The end is nigh-light and your occupancy remains a ratio (solely). What if I'm in love with chiropractic? Does that mean the logo will be apt? I sense your chicory young beverage has excused the papal vio-lect, or waited (un)seen.

No more Romeos gloat over gypsum lunch, conventional trails faking out the rib. Numerator, roman à clef solstice on the Vax-D plateau. The go-away-Minos cries no one plucks your fluoride craters, culinary prenups rinsed with metha-done and OJ.

Om is sitting and not waiting. Sitting and not venting. Aching without aching. Om is Gnostic. Om is rate hike without rate. Line dancing drops to still shot. Inasmuch as no vocabulary rides the *right here* coast not coated clef-free staff and also staves.

Krishna is moth, stuck-up headlines rub the in-crowd nirvana. Tingling for its savior. Hatchet light, a moth dialectically peeled, eviscerated by marketwatch burial lock stock & hemline farce snuck under moth's prey. Latchkey IRS square dancing bullfight *capo*.

Look at the not-look, see water be watched. See tutelage betrothed to string theocracy, see lingua franca bore down into tuckpoints. Other than the other slight new airy feelers why not vane the header toward a breath instead of wind so usual. Pressed into tone.

Jackpot: a causal weather of provincial roosts, habanero the dictatorial flytrap hello kitty scabbing preposition, hospital cornice, harvest. Wailing wall succor trims the nonplussed index. Footer creeps along towpath the low pressure holiday, a blowing forth, a ballast.

Soprano seat time crimps the flow through of the walleye tempted merely once beyond despair. The man with T imposed has tried to go away. One has afforded succor prior to this new. Along the pathway, life force has given way. A holiday comes last. And then.

Piano is the ivory a cuckoo plays its extinction to, force of m.p.h. and trident strike. Covalence doused in forest. Shampoo, a perpendicular descent. One had to look the meaning of it up. Cats hate mirrors, the opposable self. November is late again.

Having heard mellifluous enormity delivered on the white keys, she sprinted as though posing to include the flats and sharps. What short hair on the opposing cat. Feast of Saint Cecilia and the loss of John. The Gaelic form of the maternal grandmother's name.

Her charm, harried, rests in thoracic melody. The snowplow of dejected first place ribbon at best, an uneventful blue on diving-board aerobic downside to inheritance. Nasal kiss the rejected ankh of her arabesque at the hundred year watermark, a lip gloss famine.

Pressure to and from the lips arrests fine closure. Loss is benched by water. Every hiss apparently evens the s/core, but yet a formal avarice neglects imaginative force. Gross amperes threaten to revive the gloss of forth, although we know the hoards indemnify.

Accelerant beam a middle way endows, disembarks, flees its shore for third. Inquest. Feathering blank, blinks, thinking entraps the choir at zero-hour talking point debacle. One crisp run commandeers the ruthless tote bag reflected eye's last trip to the altar.

What I want to know is, asked the wielder of the scimitar, *do you date?* The wavelengths glyph their way through deerlights' head, and flexible "rip" doormats stand in for the balking points between two monocles. *When you have finished stalking . . . .* Allow me to

induce, incur a gem of touch, murmur, fend off, con your mistress (likes / dislikes / crimes). Blue's in bed too, a route fork-in-the-we'll see whatever napkin acrobatics suit embrace, dress up an axe, antler edge pussyfooting around blacklist, the *wipe your*

ashtray closing line prevaricating nomenclate that pinches frost (*is that you, honey?*) connectedly alighting upon Anchor Wat with little recollection, brittle ledge, fruit-dotted puncture, quasi-tincture after follicles go free post-brace, past surety, to bond with grace.

Scamper the deadline is blonde but dearly and beloved and sincerely yours *wa-what* is marked as Sago absenteeism, chronicle of lichen IX, crumbs for marinade, herky-jerky sparrow dips its beak into pigment catch-all, clay pigeon's affable ascent on the lam.

Palms absorb the rum brunette, I guess, then scatter lay-by to the *pull* impulse or so raid hastens and the silver yes ekes into wrinkles in the clear *I hear* of ratatouille sent home to lamb bake in the London patch of eyes assembled to paper the impediments of these.

Yes scratches its Sunday rash of botulism rituals, collagen and perfectible Luddite confirmation hearing into captain's log. The acidic ruble of basic nightlife sounding *all clear* in stairwell 5. Father curtailment, judged privately by *act now or else* savoir-faire.

Factotum fractures acid test. *Revise.* Forensic empathy contrives. Life drawing lacks class, having parsed the mood swing moldy as in brackets are the privacies we hatch like sylphs almighty, grafting winter into fatherhood, as if to have curtailed meant *watch.*

Sanitarium of grail. Action-packed. Stopper a ring- will you please - affect - a role. How so if you map the squalor of its heyday, dyspeptic interview, the editorial trigonometry snipes at passersby, corners *Maat* grimly advantaged as cousins consult chilling odds.

Aptitude can measure (reassure) view *lagra* as an editrix gives semblances their laudate. Crimping speed traps offer antonyms to ring toss just as gender gradually erodes, or do the disadvantaged come to map the torsion any fast time soon?

Citronella fastens to the ocular yardage, Fargo's eh, ah, uh— why nap can't proceed though it wishes, shirks the privet, white eases in. Wisk stuffs the warning, farming prongs electrode motherhood, forty stews on hopped-up consciousness, epilogical.

Tripods collapse, right? Huff right off into the quick(sand) &&& farm team comes to heap bright big halt. Irking admirers of the inking do a tap of wither. Why not come down to work three jobs? Why not whiten tear drops to look pretty in the card trick dried collage.

If plungers scrap the race of syringe, put it to the screws, infamy & doe. If snow buckles under bales, the indomitable *canto somnambulo* where you remembered skulking across a platypus' bill, upwardly vocal, filming at leisure the vatic dictionary of dashes: S-O-W

It was a third (of the) right sleep. Listen against the shore crossing this way to walk where ash also. . . to vocalize is to impeach. The letter of raw fiction practices amid low crews. *Per omnia secula seculorum.* And low-cal So Cals fallen RAM, even to go.

Pernicious interstate eschews 80s drama. Cable access exudes dating failure from the tin fire I-am-not-a-crook / hula hoop teaching soldier on stowaway layaway? broken plywood desde erratum. Na+ is an element at which the cardiogram sniffs.

Able bodied errata coin a fern to live above the ire. What morning reaches comes to seem a way. A card game loops around state ploys until membranes soldier on. The fundament includes these elements: safekeeping, fractions, correspondence courses . . .

Bridge over earache cups the refinery crackle unties yellowjacket's bleary rig as it ogles sunrise pulp apologizes for its pair of *ews*. First response no greater general coating paranoia gruffly tows the antecedent. Democritical tract / byline freshens up.

Fine tall swatches of lack rear seminal bleat. Untoward effacement dangers as no verb can plummet to the risen fluff as sedentary overview. The logjam fractures otherwise. Is running water free. Pronounce me when you've nothing else to take from sleep.

Disgruntle as a form, a figurine of bivouac, all their / these exposed heads, dismantled. Swoosh into how's your father doing with that conditional diagram *ah to reverse* the stalemate serfdom, whitehorse pike, rubber duck polluted by aerial dye, confessed to.

No longer easy, tryptophanic priors leech the cold play of the ply left from each diagram. Unless is symbol, or the dried wood salt gives fess. Line drawings cloy. *Are you a breath mark?* Give grace extrasensory retort. A mine field of opinion, none worth violets.

Invasion is easiest, eustachian put-it-to-bed, *pat pat pat*: this is voice. It's all in theater, dis re- tract what you've stayed, trans- instantiate commute or immune me, medicated strait of Gibraltar stipple the fort, no pace left daggered. Fare thee well. Drink the point.

Correlate collapse with strips of mica. Tendencies infine their way through. Medics, soon abrupt, leaving a close-up at the level of an ore. Ironic as shelved bed light. Called impregnable associative unction snared to reason with the tempted flat. This bruced.

Trotting, framed, the macaw is feeble on advertisement, but better to get there! Pulse is bulky, adored. Don't force the push-pin medallion in or have the vermouth tabled (i)(n) definitely. Oh it's bright again a.k.a. flip-flop sonometric microbial additives of loudmouth.

Capsize the dent, excise impertinent abduction. Silhouette of carapace. Why not inflate, defect, loquate, reply? The eminence lifts spears where spirits were. Microbes reverse position until Mass is solemnly over. Who wins? Verdant breeze. Indicatives and spree.

Goes deaf sprinting the last mile or woe. The you is meaningless. The parked spoon barely emigrates in time, *papers*. You have this need to revelate, dismember unsociable remarks. Vacation spent bloviating cloud-seeders, *poor baby*, sigh. Well-said, it's honest.

Runes ditch our salvation. Stop. Élevé's my fave you can drive right up. Sociable stop. Then obviate. Stop seeds. Now sigh nigh unto. Well, duplicate, then. Rations can be rationally conceived. I dreamed I was in leaf guard rinsed to stir until the rasp. My voice.

If then maybe perhaps yes circumstantially— near the Orkhon River, a talis manic feather entrusts us (picked last) that rope, nearer to choking whose demeanor stood up to the riches of clerical error, its critically paratactic sex (plesiosaur).

Stacked up to earwig ratchet back lexical heat mean picket thatch akimbo Norse made in Columbia (why not) trust the itch to beat the null set at choke cherishing as malt knows Maltese ne'er do welcome home error to clear the everlasting air.

Which is more bitter, hops or being thankful for what you haven't been able to do with oneself, mumbo jumbo which is always abused upright by some torrid malapropism which is sucrate, a cross-town rebuttal, falconer by default, to assassinate the warming.

Look up(right) to fix the neck (played on the old) props reused and gratitude unmeasured is mere altitude (false start). Sucrose tattles via gumbo every hankering when poached is glib, remind me to tell you about the time (remind me all the time) these spokes . . .

The mercies (merry this, merry that) handwashed and starched, a pluperfect ceremony. Sound barrier suborbit, who has time? Verbose recline or battle the upset pubescent catcall wishing our metadata invention of the pact away from newfound ringtone.

Scratch that torrent, block that kick, depreciate that cap, and hover. Downside, cluttered with upside chaff, until pound sterling rises from under bed. Leave the dimensions to us. An inclination surfaces pertaining to kissed infancy toward reelection siring fate.

Flail the floral batch process thick as piñata. He jogs in courier type, reserved, will be performing shortly the Santa Maria bipolar Plymouth rupture, a quilt by fits and starts to leak unclaimed prize (who sunk whose lips touched, E-5) voted off the island by chance.

Polarity is therapy enough. The easy listening absent whipstitch charts an elongation blithe as Surrey and as feast. Big lunk of a gent equates to moderate success in the world of logjam and in focus comes the courier with packages to parse as if and only . . .

Equanimity is the rule ruing rather than jumping to recreation, dial should recreate the witch hung to 59th parallel— how conquest is satiety. Fig debunks the tree on which duchess is quadraplexed, hogtied architecture, hums "four," receives an F, a hole in 0.

Miraculous stun guns cobble together would-be poised positions. Trance is dance minus freedom to vary from tree to shining. Limitless prig jaundice motions to the pallor in fair trade. A radical disjuncture pries some vellum from the taupe appearing (still) in threes.

Like scutwork and inferior arrests for proposal, comp (e) isition. Munition dump fire glances on reggae & salsa with celebrity judgment. In the great field, matching is in deed lost, won't you strong-arm me to the dinner table or Porta John, sublet grace.

Find collateral modernity in strength. In numbers, table the port. Match point celebrates reggae until the lance is glassy-eyed have faith work miracle mush(room). Dine with me, derange the race, give grace to pose and winter here amid the treetops close to thee.

The rhizome stupefies. U-length of a one kiloton gown. Almost anyone shocks on spec tour de _____ colorless boon. He was half in the bag. J.C. gentle as a cactus divorced from the new H_2 / over tea / an itsy bitsy nuclear sprint. Why the ivory-billed doesn't balk.

Roundhouse locus. Shipshape happen(stance) half in shock treated to nuclei walk steadily in too few rune-lengthened opiates. *But I digress.* The children of the cacti roan in craft renege on broom dusk on account of of of print-based half-tix as if only . . .

Accenture is the language of recession, frost, at attention on the puck shot photo hunt gallery's happy hour castanet (-eda). *I wish the verb refused me.* The prom charged double for all-access regalia or Cocteau's desert is bluffing, so why stand in line to lose?

Rosters fuse with thought of rosters fused with loss of stature. Do you read me? Proms spawn full regalia, *and much, much more.* The cock crows three in rows and wrists exude charged toss of the dye-cut Prospero with blades turned wings (I guess).

Vacillate all you want, this is a politics of sunlight. The decision to list names like padded feet on a gangplank, pomp and what? Wrists were made to be the blunt instruments of oceanic crossing guard need. As in I need flight, I need sleep (I know).

Ice light. Veer light. Tripartite. Wristicuffs delay the lure of pomp. Are you all shoulders? And is winter viable? I think I need the leap to have been made last year? Yes? When oceanic wilderness defrays the frost on desert lands, don't even mention instruments.

Cuisine is the crisp alarm mistaken for your protest. Who is who one pretends to be something other than a radio. Begins at creation, one calendar day: ¾ shoulders all hips. Blacked out, downhill, a foot of snow on you, concrete as Buffalo, wrists just so.

Taken tests tends to be agitating crated one to fourfold whispers. Crafted to innate *just so* alleviating whimsy until fashion tackles Crete in motion (slow). Who is alarmed? I am alarmed. Who is unarmed? We are an item. We are half low, we live long in escrow.

Hampered by molars, with exception. Note: moles have underground lab results, look, privatize your cloud design. I am blinking, not typing, not gathering mold in a Socratic up-yours *this is a test* weapons system non-escape clause unchecked box kind of way.

Craft differs from charity in what divisible young integer? I'd say the wave flows three times more than linked arms. The druthers holed up in a cloud begin to show their gravity. Once more a Midwestern afternoon I am afraid will wither. Being thus numbed.

For a taste of parity (this = this). Perilous, squamous, to say the least. No D-day valor at horticultural reformation. The flicker is dent, *ferklempt* is futile, appellate utopia. Born compressed. (de-) . . . that comes afterward. To prove effigy is sturdy, first, in stoles.

Story-ful wrongful disch- unremedies the work. The dream, the drought, the brimming qualifier scorned / pressed / copious until one peril equals two that equals fortitude. No alphabet's the same as numerator, and no sponge full-times its way through thirds.

Bait-and-switch irrigates baby talk (October 23rd or bust) a caloric hour / scratch-decoy. To be deposed is hope. A hackneyed champ's first instinct is comedic. Neither spells Friday the same under surveillance. Saying this hinges on borrowed hole-punch fourths.

Watch the trough, display hack hampers in media res to spell the veil within gesticulating uncle-state. The four of you, the five, the ditch pose calls out rust. *One calorie or two?* The lumpen say-so window row row rows to bait the sixth. *Was that you to the north?*

Nothing human here. Remains of X. More accurate as preacher: in the middle of you no one hears the cedar fall until it gulps, standing dunes against the maw. Years are ad infinitum collected ruckus, ferreted out. Here's the muzzle of sign language, oars lost.

Reach or middlemake the loop. Fallen to bits in signatory shelving. Trounce the opposition in spare parts. As sacrificed as water is, the roar of fishing gloms onto an inaccurate portrayal of the rucksack. Is this yours? Lost filaments glide into lumbar.

Close call. Nothing gives its intake. The slurry wall bites back, overcompen-sates, is final, recanted. The *I-did-not* for the *I-might-have*, electrolyte (anger) whose run-off masquerades as involuntary preview & advantage, where input fairs well, a truce.

Ruses from this vantage point light range. All intake's fastened, steep. Compensatory *dommage* incenses the argument. All squalls drive grasp. The tendency to thrive gives back. White calves view sack. Tachometric fins replay the radar's scope sequentially.

Maître d' as ordered observes eminence as mandala opposite cohort. Or peep, bloating club's dotage capitalizes every T until works project stops, fully tender booth, beacon uphill loitering minus fromage. Origin of big bang counterpoint locks quarters evasively.

Gin's tepid. So am I. The t-bills make no green unless blue is considered (green). No longer toothsome, every novel fill is moat-like. Peeps give gravy reputation. Be what you will, the lute is loutish and the cheese goes wild. I think a clang is clever. Can we cope?

If fogs abate. Two nymphs grace a ski plane, faster than foreclosure. The first one said you are not clean, but red is my favorite passage, *no*? Homespun. Play for keeps the coq au vin is paraffin, diagram is gripe, ven is illness. Ring, stir, until the mile kicks in.

Composure's a sniper's dream. Pick a card, any crawlspace. Trim the ask until disclosed. The first one of the frogs drank grog. And now? Diagrammatic peril skates past you. A waxen grief remains critique. Sombreros do not hide (us). Keepsakes wither.

However one floats, aggravates the scheme, pyramidal, kitschy, sedentary, asleep. Glass glints among insulation brick-road breathing flatly where and when cerveza preens fret the handsome bogs, laced blade mourns a bull's-eye pandering a la carte.

Sleep veers into locus. And the target is no target at all. The cards flash past, and with them, all the keeping in reverse. Revered roads wreathed with silver give the weeds their floral due. The grating progress is a low, and with that, flat (perhaps) abiding.

Whether substitute counteracts supplement, rated (raided) by county, age, gender. Bland bionic photo whose fur print distends the flower's credenza. Tweet, sings her hall pass tracing mild snow. She culls a suite, orders cursive rain, packs a magazine.

Photosynthesis differs from photo radar, in what way? Wheat stings joints. See the one behind the perfect shade tree, singing counterpoint? That's the one you want to watch be swift by curative curses, thumbing through a magazine, thinking Ascension Thursday.

Gluten or therapy, always knowing where the camera is situated, pledge of glut, cover up the graded foible. As if Jeremy had it in for the swing set, gambling on a letter, better yet, a ditch. Rainbow voodoo as one meditates, self-medicates, praises the non-breath.

Listen to the squeak of swing go back and rev forth. Repeat. To grade, ungrade. Improve just pulsing. Anybody out there from the east end? Get the camera, ra, and let me *singular* this medi-space (to taste). And cinnamon be non-, neat nutmeg. Here.

Of a god, the rust walks on water, floors crack under the skeeball of surreptitious heel. What complies, a straight Medivac line? The racial profile of a harbor, sleek with product placement, ping and duck, coughing up location, petroleum rip of least familiar spice.

Skeet shoot flurries. Bar no pisces. Duct tape ramps up the already taut place close to water. Complicit, owned, dovetailing, petro-glissandi let rip keyboard spills undocumented as these lined propeller vox pop rack and pinion clashes about rust . . .

Their pall scant hoots the mocktails. Scar-of-place, hypodermic crate of lemons, corn stiff from abduction. Or else. Dew freezes when proofing the hi-horst (coefficiency). What's reinforced: *I am destined outward, star puts shin to star.* Regresses to aviate, sic.

Lockers rife with force, due diligence, and shifted water. Puts to proof the Orson in your Welles. Deprive me of something out of feathered tar. Release the coefficient dappled in an ornery wave. Non-tending tension tines allows the fork to scar. Succumb to lace.

Assurance spins orbit off-road. Searching for the right body part, this addictive hint. Obstinate fertilizer, upper limits, how much you might lose. Bankrupt(see), amber memo lightbox yes/no brink as plus, red minus. Up or down? It's museful. a-mused, B-listed.

Tropes liberate when tinkering deflects only the rational. Rupture's like that amber bead about to blow apart engraved roadway. See Jane muse. Be witty. Memorialize tints effected through addictive grazing. Point click paint pint printerly. The body is a part.

Interloping abbreviates a.m. Aphasia shuts down fringe, pro-jects. Breakup esta noche! Gently reapply the throng after three hours. Rub into skin. She does that well, thinking onto a subject. Inkjet roadside diction with artificial counts. Stun the gamut for once.

Fridge rubric overloads the jet. Indicted skin does well mid-century (where are we?). Dumb luck is first off dumb. Thinking deserves a subject subjected to no thinking, but a heart, what is that? Three or so counts wedged between the blades of iffy staves.

A smidgen of delirium (toxin) at the behest. Hookline impairs back-to-the-past. Truncated merry go nowhere. At the biconcave call, eagerness and theocratic rapids of cholesterol amend the *go seek and I'll find you* else we wave off panic.

Sinker after wallowing. Call cave shored up. Eager to delay the critic mending waved upon panned oxen. If you pin the find on all you've lined, there will be rapture. Close the test of taxes. Where the (e)king shivers. Keep the faith that hope has carted.

One axle departs, then two, skitter of deposit, surfeit courtesy. The wan thumbs-up humbled graft. Vaccinated against cyan festival. Grape wine strips account violation from crudités. So goes the luck 'o the bait, refined. Liposuction gears its rebound to win.

Vibrant rubs vivace the wrong way. Cyan a ra when he speaks north. The Violins are bound to part our ways. A surfeit of luck yields spatula this, sprig of the la. Contained, refined, invisible haste remembers cork days at last halt. So now the gears seem rum.

Fabulous and reactual, acting up, no entry 6 am to 6 pm blabs *karnak*. Apostrophe on dust jacket election. Take back your barb, grounds for ceremonial tag-out. *Le chimera l' occitane.* As if shears made the wool unwieldy, sharp as pinot in the year of the rabbit.

Post-print jacket dust immersed in further lust now in arrears. The wall paint hurts the wielding as years of habit norms. Entreaties nip the lab coats and the *noh*'s revered for what? Acting is not likely to come up. One fabric might mean two for six. "Discuss."

Chatroom covets the prance hot-tin of approbatory hush-hush. Agape pattern figures into ransom. Spears pontentiate custom of clatter. Eleventh hour sets its thermostat to 1. Attack lets go its bureau-spackled hymn. Mark to market pelt, no vacancy for straggler.

Rancid period of probing chapter eleven rivulets makes latte sour. The thermo-matic vagrancy affords the spackle, just as tack taken comes to seem haute couleur. And strange figurines presumed young shush the old by being close to covetous.

A skype hypnosis in which panhandles execute a last will, flour-rich safety deposits percolate the same words over and in (yawn) po' *em* denies lettering. Impugned RVs revoke daylight savings, can you spare a cycle, the ramen wheel, freeze-dried pall.

Psychic prowess genuinely endears me. Letters enrich and venerable daylight eases me from bed until the saved piece ripens and stays handled even as the Gnostic gospels wring our hands for us, revealing points of will that flourish under conditions ideal.

Shiite kick howness is friendly & interjects a seam. Fetters pull up britches generally my fright appeases serial dream behaving all a piece. I scandalize heave acrostic vespers sling power from its sand purpose, teeming out of joint Marrakech stumps the frivolous.

Matins sling the shot put and propose. Esteem's a value in this joint. Cross words become one, and she puzzles over fetters to evoke a seam. A friend is someone you can please. However means objection's merely prone. Frivolity's simple zone.

Quiet as trade paper emeritus, creation: do you take, will you swear, fennel faints the 3-down and 10-umbels across / ova patience now! black square phenom, you're playing this for whom? Special counsel to the argument eroticizes a pink, eros weighs her down.

Stalks umbilical lease summer back for stints and quash the blackness trading on a pink beneath that weighs some cross like act. Phenomena portray winced odes as if hall paint had resembled the qui vive on which we are unlikely as patience will be squared.

Hell-bent stiletto (no valentine) calls up reserves stacked shoes subsume a memorial. Defamation is pacifist-ish polls sumo Mt. Somewhere. Racquetball court fellates the ribald megawatt. Turpentine emasculates the stub by an infraction of seven inches.

Straightedged sumo pax tries wattle for a mask. The snubbed fact of infraction enters depth as a reserve study, tacking on the veil of innocence where ignorance once wheedled from a saint once bathed in turpitude in a pre-cert way (two mints in one).

Fasten or haggle, it doesn't much matter, fact is broom to bellow waddles in optometric breath-fresh mischief, in a plutonic but fatal sense, further than *no fumar* breaks china critical errors are coded open, Samsonite cradle spurns admission couched in checklist.

Room service arrives beneath steel. A casserole is inadmissible, despite the crouched position of headlines. Errata-prone denominators sporting plutocratic shoulders ought to fume when they are told. Hagiography attests to multiple contributors along the cistern.

Goliath mulls over diagnostic dictaphone. Flexing high-jumps reheat AP medial devolution. Burns the burr off dim / hi / low, stokes the Lasik tribe. For if today air went dead, one out of 15 would drink topaz from the masthead, percuss a pearl.

APB's been issued for a ribcage left not far from here. *Were you present when your picture was taken?* Diagnoses trim our expectation, cussing out the high for being jumpy as a cat(fish). Lumped into the drink are bits of B-complex to keep things paxy.

Taken last, issued where, all seafood eventually dips as bar room malfeasance (the phototypical generic marathon minute-cide). Hostess curtsies curates the register's boil. Cash on credit bumps the C-grade energy life into fax jam. Call for back-up soon.

Crash the course. Extend curt seas to desert lands. All hands on reckless mutts, oil feathered in the street under the soda lamps. *Which -cide hurts one more than the other?* She was a dandy lass, said he. A foody, blast-from-the-past kind of a gal.

Thy airmail in a wind-up doll, prime jangle. To euthanize a patient bloodlets smites by confession, how she might drain the swamp under non-compete gratis. The one they peg for roadside overturned smoke and cries, on-duty for queen's day, beside -empty-

Welcome to the confessional. Please speak slowly, and state your name, your favorite sin, the smitten eminence of targets, and the duty shoes in which you dance then cry. A non-compete clause winds up airmen. Therefore, euthanize before filching jangles.

Dollhouse falsetto, I know have met the acquaintance of birds jackals from crow leaflet mole refuge. Two-step where one slides up against adjacent girlfriends, dirty "in the flesh," pros same as bronchial cons unfairest dogfight, speaking is laceration, bilking us.

Trump the wildlife via rows of centrifuge. Fare better than the lance, bilkish as figurative dirt (figurines) adjacent romp. The fugal met means quaint steps through white birds. Leaves are risen falsely. Constancy fogs peaks. The us in use conveys faint thirds.

The worry is world-proof, weirder than punitive sightings. The shipbreaking beaches pallbearers in paradise scintillated, deplorable, the way bans go, moratoriums, the hunter's prolapse. Inveighs windmill / what hinges on. Ant: do parks need possessives?

Line drive breaks live run. A part of speech is quiet, if not pure. The dice are spun, my own, your bearing up under the strain. My sense of sight, your beach head, my mill town rungs, your hunt. The world proves what it is each morning. Scenery never to disband.

A run-up on poppyseed, rough houses, drill sgt. applies yes sirs no ma'ams (snake eyes) let's ramble forward skull / crossbones (bows? as on— no is the reverse). Cred is short for come on party people, not in address only but *dear* is laughable. See exhibit A.

A day of hope ("stand on your toe") as in dress code premises some violation's violet. Even bones go cross where poppies fill the field blousing its way across as far as sense of sight can tie the drill to yes and credibility, the long and short, the run-in, the clear.

Count on candid excuses, Babel or a turnkey. Last week's crass Windsor knot acts constitutionally bland, up to the steep (sleigh bell) before Oz, an even keel is far more indiscrete vs. a scram(bled) *look out* a prerogative. The wait's less obvious.

Soaring blots make bland shadows in the sky. Unchimed with sleigh bells and the keening swept beneath the bled fathoms urgently filled by acts of tres-. The dimes are rolling in, and sheep are holding. Urban won't meet rural anywhere, nor blend.

Bots among the living handswift glides ↓. Port-au-Prince cabal deals white alkaline requiem. Punta Cana bequeaths unto a trader his twinkle, though not his trait? police the penny giveaway. Boxcar transit instance quits the special victims unit season two.

Accordingly, the trade's a wink from instances of seasonal vitality. What givens prattle in the bottom of a pail? Canon boasts transition not at all. The living dread mung beans. These heathens gone ballistic box up wrinkles to delay inevitable crime scenes.

How it rankles, the more you think, the louder a cliffhanger blurts out. No worries. Wisely in the pick a bale battle of hay mode, throttle up for caffeine divulgence your made-in-Budapest toupee treatable incoming declared at customs spayed e-tablet.

Vise fits right between two larger bales. The rotten troupe gives customary pavement hangings, rank and file alike. Round battle zones keep threads in bed. No matter outside seems so hurried. Thinking comes to work screeching. Besides, no one listens anymore.

~

No one no one no one the echo. Squeeze play begins with j and ends with o. They are small letters drooping from the scaffold. Proud parent of the fix-is-in. So incompetence should not curry the field, somewhere a heat on its own quashes ram horn, flings it up.

Rent goes skyward. Competence curries *por favor* or else a rash gins up the lace in folds and lets ride droop and chaos. Queasy shoulder-height parental stories wind up mounting a disgrace campaign. The *is* diminishes in proportion to reality released.

Hold Buy lord of all land-locked Branson habitats. Rent and –ent, its ancestor: best when flu (curse?) is alliance. Cold, cuter when bayoneted. Time wrinkles in dollar bill win lose stand-up sit-down the biggest liability. Jam band farm aid swatches, game over.

Curlicues are born, not made. The cutting board resists the arm and on my watch the lame flog ampersands the way that entropy used to park. The kinks have worked their way up out of sit-ins, and some canvassing has had to happen after guns met butter.

Trundle down the plastic enemy pair. Serrated is the euphemism for swarm. Duraflame blogs its sauntering mantle, to do away with antique as descant, the slippery premium. The tendency to stare into a sink. All bulletins and under-the-door fraudulent cheer.

Air rates durable with staring. Pink bulletins floor one being daunted by serrated edges. Armloads of slipknots offer peril to an enemy without a name. *Let's go sailing* for posterity. The tended masquerade means lasting peace up in the beige clouds.

Postmark in chit-chat. Get me the bell out of a hook. Attempt a triple bök off the high dive pale, limps a championship c.) dispersal of rounds. The spinnaker presents what it can, this aqua, *agua* prepares for X-Y-Z, but won't outlast. ACME colors clip the nimbus.

Purse strings (rings) outlast the pared clips. Parsed nines, hyped quips. Ship shape champs line up the chits, the chimps stay pining between rooks. Cooked eel mimics reel-to-reel aquatic slumber that might hit the mark along the lines of postures marked.

When you wing it, the fat outwits you. There's a space (insert here) the lingo owns the vertex by the hair of its chin. Signs "banana" or "vehicle" interoperably. The bone brings a nicer prison. Price is afterward, mine detonates extremity, lovash, a saucer of olives.

A nicer person vents alone. Mines elude most saucers. O lives longer than Q: why? If one of us is hinting, certainly the other will become inane. If heresy, what next? The pace of fat is wing-free, maybe that's why inserts get deserted very fast. Air's still owned.

Nice line, but too much float, bleacher, like Sago, no dividend. The gloating rhinestone procures. Reduce the fryer, scoot plainly to your weddings, the best heretic nibbles carefully into the host dye #80. Sack a village you'll never soar over. Mosquito cliché.

Dryer weather floats the puck across division problems. Lodestones match their gravity, and rinds tossed out of windows long since lost their sack. The oars of yore are quitters, and the dings add up at nuptial blasts. Red dye number what's its name scoots past.

Lodestar dexterity, who challenges a rink when the skaters have shunned the muck, smashed a thermometer, reordered or burned their family albums. One photomosaic overdoing it means the grin slips. A ranch is a fine place to rest a hydrophilic insect.

Stuck in more meter renditions, families burn skates. They photograph the opposite of rest. They run in threes. The sour mash that defines them grips the shun-gun of the hydroponic overdose while grinning slows the bait. A chalice would be nice, or slip.

Succotash. Maize. Amazed at burning. Mirror, mirror. Magnesium (while alive) gets into a tiff over moonlight, one up on the same putrefaction. One keeps the words this way until they disintegrate, takes a shotgun approach to its introverted rite. Fallacy of white.

Shores purify the world. What roaches live on vert? The foibles of the fractions leave their wavelengths high. They integrate moonlighting with the family silver. They leap over pampas grass. They take a minute to be floral, then they wimp into the life force.

It's no Parnassus, no revolute cycle. Mother mooches off her cut-and-run carnival lily a gulley will be appearing as protean gullet mish-mosh. Pig latin moisture will back up the perforated casualty stretcher the nebbishy sorry lip service tasting a peregrine purple.

Other touches offer vales of fear. The gullet's still. A serviceable lip plays brass, usurping every woodwind in the storehouse. Tea and cyclicals make stocks a quaint run through with peerage clipped. The revolution is a pot of gravy. Missing parsons lap up slights.

What does the other pouch among seedpods, scrounging, do for the summit? This happens. The stemware, as if by accident, abolishes the cylcothymic dome. Earl Gray. Per quod the jumble defaces the fact of you. House on stilts crouches in a vaster foyer.

Round table conversations still the facts. Mitts make lovely destinations, following humble acts. A vast foray of seedlings yield a future face. The other appears clipped among patches of shade. Contrast might have been an accident, if not purely planned.

Luv Ya equals, oxidizes, surprises. The delphinium greens its helter-skelter axis. Snow is a human package fraught with passes, come-ons, exits, luck. In your pitstop blanket jackknife. Live to see *you're it*. One might not grasp the co-anything of rinsed silverware.

Recent stop lights tag the rascal of a habit burning the x-axis, thereby greening other plates that hack their way to raspy dugouts where the rinse is splayed. Command posts now give sifting back to oxidation. Penny at a time, the any of these wares left out.

Belated brakes go-seek the private out-channel. Man overboard. Nook of liar liar. Linedam zoo story. Children hide where stitching strikes low and away. Walkie-talkie best friends forever is tedious as the hold button pacifist ignoring last-minute 1¢ spark.

Boarding schools are full of nooks. By contrast, airy zoos hide ways-through minutes and deep tedium before breezy pacific holdings overdo the channel while hide-and-go-seek is played out the best of ignorance. Saving's not the same as earning, any day.

Who does what we do when I-do sputters. Hock the ducat and bring the elephants out to gratify. Heed the warning sign of factory silo refilling its no-money-down pyre. Back up the earth to ignore anthrax smiles. The extent to which one is backward, treading crude.

Luck would have the razing past. The Tories glean whatever's pre-pyre. Lack of earth endures, while backward rude goes straight to glue. The silos multiply omnivory. The phantom lung vests do their stories straight from trash. Leaders on the docket thrash.

Flour *psshhh* water equals double the opera. Sun cont'd. Come in you must be chilled to the teeth. Come out you must be in kindergarten, under her thumb (a Mrs.), coloring. Punisher, square footage, polar as futurity. Amen meets omen in the antiquated field.

Here is the kinder part. Small amid the leafage and double the happiness. The sun warms teak, and worlds come by. Chill weather quietly disintegrates inside. The color of young becomes a polar field. An opera gives grace to otherwise, when gently fielded.

Is it ending? Has it ended? Does panic scathe the 2 pm skin, stroke of fiction. Let's bail out. Why, not when. Drug-free zones each November school year embroider your pill. Pentacle sulks inside echoTV. Wristband exonerates noise, demanding its throat back.

Friction shows the population skulking around back alleys inconveniently positioned behind buildings. Sending violations throughout lighted and unlighted corridors, the sample frees the portent of selected echoes. Noise unequal to embroidery prevails.

Misread, overload has tried understatement, packaging. Laramie with less homes on *the* endangered *show*. Marie's head conversant playing hooky dark to dark, near somebody the bored dispatcher free from all caps shouting, boycott this funeral. Blink in, out.

Lower case verse dispatches headlines to a pack of automatons. Homes range from dark in to dark out. Reading groups overtly reason with their captors, plunked in the midst of danger wearing veils of ignorance. Crawling to the center statement, certain.

Not an aside? Odd, how a sure thing gouging p(low)ing *ow wow ow* sounds cheerful as the carebear gelatin assembly line ditch they toss your extended family in. Craft is a shopping bag for the clap your hands stomp your feet skit sagging with the indoor temp.

Lapping up the vintage, one de facto ditches class. The family extends, raftside. Hopping into gelatin, berating individuation. Posses of neglect mount up. There are insatiable self-heedings. Whose assembly do you vouch to skeet shoot toward the grave?

In the blackgreenredblue brickyard, sampling your Bonaparte, pièce de résistance: bass or cod finning its way *vunder* as in *vunder*ful stream, exclaim, congeal or conquer. Hand-me-ups don't attain excrescence. Presidio strangles the bayneck. Foot in the maledictus.

Part of one streams through the presidio. Another bays with querulous dreamers on demand. The cod immerses ample feeling in an intellect, no-holds-barred toward handouts of the *very* kind. A wonder to evict the stains from bricking out the upstarts.

Part two soaks the answer. Paint by numbers avenges screenplay instills the do or die. Water peaks, criminally fills the volume changing fly for protein, batch pimps *grrr* from the gentle as she goes you can do it symposium. Seventh wonder is loveless. Was.

~

Numb barometers act on play, posing as less than printemps. Shelter flies out of the screen. The criminally sane offer diurnal peace. Flecks of water downsize change. The thrift appears genteel until you fill out forms on oaken desks as search and rescue.

Dependency on polite fact. It hurts this hurts let it go from the skeptic's pat-a-cake lure. One-a-day smirk, a dossier riddled with beginnings. The companion guide you are from source affirmation. Upscale the projected figure. The siren shrugs off *sincerely yours*.

Firm as *firma* and to scale lit. Kept patricians lure the vulnerable reupping all the time as if gin were unlimited, with murk. The turtle dovelet springs from mind's neglect and ROM's no matter. *Her constant companion was the incompetence of others.*

The sherpa squirms (inquisition) Stockholm must be burning. Easily your *opus dei*, proof + moonshine blind, not as much a quirk. Stale garnish squibs the kick, shines a vector twenty times filtered speed, remedial and scrawny straw inters the tap dance to a loss.

Pale face surrounded by pale light. The quibbling brought on by gloss endures. Proof disintegrates reality. Quick draw media fronts for stocky urns. The quizzically drawn shade filters the dress code blind. Quirks fall from armature like some used blouse.

Bodice drizzled with lace, a motel sequence, face-down in the pumice garage. Evening is Re: pharaoh not poesy. The holstered feeding wavelink is privy to the clip-on february whose pride parades undresses platters insolent sounds a cinctured opening state.

Dice make licensed doilies spring to life with riveting ascension. Links to teak ride reputation to quiescent leaves. The clipped reversion to a dress code elicits peals of laughter where the scythe would be. Waves chime right where we look for evening.

The time-out does not scoff or complain as much as pour into manila's fourth "if" crests cubbyholed, wallows. As they say. Move is *said*. A raving. The bell's coptic secrecy tint is ground zero pulp for hour's convincing, untucked, flirtatiously large for 4 a.m waking.

There was a mantilla, too, with prayer. Coptic breath to take the raves and charge off centrist scoffing to the unformed will. Revealed in breath and tucked in wells dug recently beneath the pulp to drive our languishing from cubbies. Low toned fuel at last.

Flotilla prepares to collect Hibernia, browse the racks, cry for soft landing, ease of emission and leftist oh something complicated wanted to be revered. Paycheck firsthand lost among them, REM sleep declared *be good or else* answer against it.

Check the backhand prior to hypnosis. Then check the swerving thumb. The pica type is all over my page. Remember hibernation left out on the track. And summer's only lexicon's a seacoast breeze at cost. No telling with the reminiscences of hacks.

An epigram in eidetic swivel. Or the thump of brake light smearing wrap-around jaws moist (must) loosen font. Point each unconscious flutter toward rosacea vase. Nest pitches into windkey. Name of which surf-like voilá crowds cloud into a picture's oils.

Pilfering another's recall clumps together lutenistic azure. The only hitch is cloud control, contraptive as the key of sea. Lalala stricture and its spoils. The shutter clocks us wrapped around the rapture of a loose tune. Epigrappling winks at newfound ones.

Lunestra stores its piqued blue as if fearful. Captivity squeezes the triggered chin. A quick hit. Whose stitches pull a contraceptive la-de-da. Last minute of a little bar. Staff held high snuffs out any mention. Easygoing foundling talk leads one to wonder.

Moon is full of sleep. Noon merely rhymes. A queasy midnight triggers hints of vigilance. Conceptual minutia blend with art. A rigged thin lift bars height that might spawn fear to middling staves. Ten hut squeals distend the distance between minerals and gems.

Ishmael reads the riot, actual reality, the soporific two by two, the bestial logo. Intrepid barbacks kneel over jetsam as in some coin-operated finish. Depravity. The selenium graft, mid-torsion. Guess glasses in the stare, animated, calling attention to the quarry.

Lasses rare mine coin-ops of a jury-proof contention. Indentured servitude shows through the torso. Riots start outside reality. A sophomore can integrate a logo into bread. Trepidation tends to show through thick glass. Animation flows once cast.

Classes are evidentiary. Half-baked descent from where one is among the judges. Service game promulgates a votive bird whose song cannot ward off blue book value. Grade A yeast, delimited by spasm, exhumes the question lurking in the thorn bush.

Value turns to inverse of pacific light, all surface, with pale quest. French horn with tiny mouthpiece offers devotions hindered by the lack of blast in pulse. The descent into the virtual meant instruments lost exotic lure. Thorn sounds are always an inherent gray.

To pacify (incur) the upside-down punctuation all things supple, armored anon alon(g) argon brass element evangelizes the mossy clime. Pandemonium disguises leitmotif. Conducive to faux pas binges on string and bow. Vane creaks, lacquering its mettle.

Laxity bridges faux this and faraway that. Lime wall paint dithers neighboring pronouncements, pacified by low stringed integers. One steps across motifs in motion slow as largo bow. Generous moss incurs a place within the intellect. A rest from what.

Transamerica ridges where crust folds under contract. The scrub is dangerous to stealth. Whole food straightens happiness, but who do they express train late to the party of two? Who receives odds on fire, acts open-flamed, friendly toward a threshold?

Rubbed lamp leaves off amp. Rate hikes dwindle, and the late train offers art at suspicious odds. Pen names rust. Ridge was never one of us. A smidge of threshing shifts the crops. Happy are those . . . who wear scrubs to the parsonage to rescue muss.

Thou salt not fear the weather forecast, wrong even (the act of) cheats its players. One is used for "I am" *the fear*— gainsay, caught digging a text black, what did you cure the stone with? No chain or name. If happily down a stream, a spotless agenda will elope.

Heat lacks pomp; spots on camera show rain shifting layers from the eye's caught act. Gains eclipsed by pale neglect seem rigged; thus, atonement's stuttered by forlorn alone beings evening the score. The ether comes to fear because we're gravitied right here.

Calliope, she swore top to bottom the news out of Darfur earned its wings, sensational as layover, bonfire. If for some reason countermeasures fail, however glib, or lore-full if it weren't for the gumption of lashes, nourished bygones would beg the reverse.

Ashen template is turned counter crevice to repeat the cyclical enactment of its liberation from existence. Segue after segue hastens itch to roust out sting in favor of the days to be invented if not measured as a part of planning the removal of the fur lengthwise.

There are two clocks in unduplicated hand, the overflow: alive and cooling ecuadorian brims crawling inward snubbing / sunbathing in warm totals of libertarian Alice. Rough segway from city to sewer to pelt. To skin a short feature, marry two ladders, fall for it.

Svelte appearing shoulders featuring an addled presence roughing it, conjures up cool living or the lack of clocking a potentially duplicitous gesture. Whatever fall brings, we are ready for the law to quiver. Sun goes shy against the skin, a total of subtle flow.

Bone licks salt. Quandary finds son closeted, rattled as shawl is aware. Stare into lift. Tingle. Dine on configurations. How one dies before it defers, raises charm, propping its thought: "chopstick" "wheelbarrow" spacious, wading, strings prana through gaiety.

One is steeled to prana, maybe, maybe not. Wind against laces helps the violet die to harm. I watch the violet never close. Uplift finagles the choir at rest. Before it does, a note helps pace stick figures as they run for safety. After wading in the still pond.

Who fakes out the warning dash or badly drawn dot symbol famous for its all you can believe. How the curtain's Artemis wept. Jack-in-the-box mixes with don't bother me now. Here's yours foolishly, air raid doubled over as downshift, sticks, glass, and mint julep.

Aching's over when the mix shifts to a double dosage of down light. Cayenne whips up raw taints. The dots are hitched, and rabble's roused, a julep at a time. Tick tock flip flop, now the caution extrasenses stop watch boxes rowing row to have, to (quaintly) hold.

Is it easier to crop the blended profile, so mournful, that she who breaks rank recycles mail sent, phishes for sample swath, rhetoric, dangles "legs in the fire" to quote the only password for skin. Let verve appear droll as mild flower quintuplet patches of science.

Towering qua vertical yards, the lending tree breaks into yawning. All around, anklets are falling to the shoes. One phishes for location thrice. Letters to comrades change the context of wild flora. Legs do well to stomp where flecks of percussion add a little flavor.

A regime chances submissive wrangling. For a fee, the scalp on backseat slumps under lesson plan, surpasses the quiet countdown. Slot parlor electrifies the loop 'n swoop territorial swap meet in part roulette discussion buries its baton of taste at the fairground.

Missives down the whooshing in the head, the tintype of an oracle. One wastes ground by bearing down on passage. Chance summations divvy up the spoils après caloric regimens begin to wind down in the roulette stirring of batons and obeying triangles.

Dismissal shuttles disappointment to the carvery. I can only be responsible for could and would and not perhaps. Would you grant shapes their loot, curlicues for a cleaner mink. All natural noose. Riot for clothing kicks off at autopark. Diverted ° stands inside.

Lean mink's stochastic, although happenstance roots out autoposses. Hand over the wood, the shawl, the rant displaced by loathing. All senators leave the world at once when shuttles leave. A craving marks the net, and oversail go mantras of the river.

Ducks in a row, fix, edit, enrich, put them back together adjourning happiness from nickel cassettes. Root against wicked adaptation. Sleep tight errand: "swell ranch" swamps reelection bid. *Gee, sir* is the sequiter, *très aural*, down arrow with strep, tongue's intro.

Reps take a gander at the sequence before dappling canvas and eventually finding sleep. A steep bid means unhappy competition, maybe. Cortisone works windows. Errand after duckbills. Enriched accompaniment, leading to an unabridged cadenza.

New lilies struggle upstream, chop-wood fantasia unwelcome as helpmeet. Café overdoses on breath. Running of the herd paints soup can pastels on delicate Tao-laden components. Night. Ever insolvent, ayurvedic, dodges the Newtonian twofer. Sorry ends.

Presence of mind eases the he/art. A ratio comforts just as vividly as silk reveals the shade. The unintended consequence of breathing is more breath. Just so, a helpmeet comes to seem a champion. Rising solvents lodge within for systematic cleaning.

Center square's jazz hand *quiz me again, you can't be serious*. A missed opportunity stabilized, is cirumspect. Tuba divided by triage trades informed consent for rent due. One flask of periodic victory lacks umph, while the other happily disinfects a standard.

Legato's warm, staccato's a short pin. Somewhere in the midrange of these brass intestines lies the form due composition. Jazz comes down to fizz. Circumlocution finds its way to staves hacked into by thought breathing. Adverbs change rhyme scheme.

-ly is the moniker, performative, macho. The spin mechanism of grade fields its trip to androgynous cymbal. Legs up, curbside state arises charged to the circular about-face, lack of glucose. Illus- (lose). E: the dessert of the abject. Nudges in, but why?

Field trips lead to quasi-this qua that. Trajectories impart a little conscience. In what why? Pin the tablet on the dong quai, perhaps? Charisma's left curbside while the circuits fill to generosity. A healing, up-close kind of a dessert gemmed with ingredients.

The attendance is momentary before what you meant to include in the *yana* stalks the widest berth or preserve (boy/girl elided, cage match) though a little bit softer. Such is what will do. To stand in front of a terminal and proselytize. Frosting or ruffle.

Preaching's work. To activate a brain share catches softness with the steel transfer of entropy, an unintended consequence. What is a moment once it's here? Age twitters while gifts filling the inbox cease to matter. Only outflow shows, is felt. As path.

Blinds a lash tweaked to be at least as joyful as the surgery that left it on the eve (eye?) everyone slows or pretends against, auctioned raw, blocked IN-stant. Fresco folds. Plaster for a limited time ekes out, exists in charge. Oyster impounds a pearl per ounce.

Law pesters freedom by inflecting it. The in-group seeks to pound the periscope into a holding pattern juried on a leash. It would appear that plaster outlasts symptoms of its lack. Joy's distinguished by its lack of preening. Every eye is destined to dismantle f/act.

Puzzle mandates the inflation. Studious, a wind tenses up. Wires kiss. Unforgiven goes yellow to black. Gretel out of bounds. Now all is over with us. Pebble greets the infantile timer. Blue slapped with script, made of crying, closet rods, open 24/7. Soft as tooth.

Lapping up the hours, one tenses. For the spared rod, behavior is inflated. Infantile humanity deemed soft becomes as terse as now. Indifference turned mandate chaps the undergone nuzzling. Toll resembles boundaries. The hovering includes moist pebbles.

Klesha, hot air squealing from what is, menu not arrow, crossbow ♂ as infinite as crib note: game of a name, exposé. I keep hearing "you know." Implements. I am glad for thinking. Replaces me better than the undo command paid with the spate of maybe.

Factual rearing tones the men. Finesse leans down into the meow syndrome, a lad might frame command post after quasi lariat domain. The air's what is. And what is not amounts to some foul note kept in the yard framed by electric fence and guard posts.

Going postal flees the coop on all fours, a purr snatches the mouse from crumb shade. Choppy seas off Cuba Libre's outpost as diamond mine. Walking it down though I recline THE FOLLOWING IS A REPORT of medicinal cadmium power stored in sunflower heat.

Leesburg's where he goes to port. *La bella* land, where princess eyes decline the lighter shades of optic mind. Imagine being lower than a flower and more natural than a hutch. If storage beaten down amounts to jewels, then anyone can rinse them, anyone can fly.

Strauss out of penitentiary blossom trades backrub for relation. She tosses among her petals *gelt* a sinew (extension dial 8 then taste the bitter crevasse). Shortchange helical drapes spun on grafted insignia. Crest ends up compact, effervescent for a raffish spell.

Change violates dimension settled once insignia afforded a perverse spell to spawn loss. Major sentences forged acquire new meaning on the sometime slavish overpass where worlds turn small from distance rubbed into reality like tensile braces poised to bloom.

Spurious and preternatural netscape coats the uterine universe. Palace of black growing on barbed catapult, last *élan vital*, a verisimilar -ness programmed. Stiff nation overshoots the " so diode must tween the ball to a state of rest and sac fly the resident newt.

Terrain makes keening sack cloth opposite of *élan*. Perhaps not universally, but oats have always clarified. Barbarous deeds are clocked in sorrow, just as underneath there seems no rest at all. A dialogue at best assimilates undying tracks within each weather.

Led into identity under 18 safety pins the flap backward. Skydarkness sympathetically sneaks grain to the gentleman. She asks him to bag the speech it nurses stopwatch pity emollient intact like the drop, the drop of what we can lose, we lose without speaking.

Shyness gets the drop on fire, until somebody's watch includes didact. Only yesterday, the peaches were a thought. It seems uneven to parse leaping for safekeeping. Sunday might have been a guess. One gentlemen equals just how many men to ward off?

Who breaks a calculation or blows its quest into a box so gentleman A may dismount? No fuss. Dandruff pits the soil as it sprinkles down. To be good enough, woman B gets away with time where Xanth is ginger, garlic, the hop / skip / jump stuffed with ever after.

Rough equivalence wrinkles the nest. Precision bests its calculated fuss. Bad as better warrants an investigation of the russet perquisites. When ginger rises to the level of fast notice, breakage happens. Low onto the horizon is a settled block where feeling goes.

Precocity depends on skin. On quarter-inch tissue wrap, lowest mountain. Premature meridian, heartbeat crescendo, maestro's failure to comply. Rallies against dumbstruck boiling point. A new wall keeps out autoerotic payola carols when the cold snap bites.

Trigonometry accounts for any decrescendo in compliance during middle years. Allies clump together just ahead of boiling over into wiggle room much needed although scarce. The only issue left is the repeat sign rallying to downbeat and the skin's vibrato.

Send/receive status, square root of daily bread. Only knowledge decoheres a colony sickens interferes battles crawl space for prime seating. One should speak frankly if May is to multiply. Odd angular line must not quaver too vastly. A fire leaves its print.

Primogeniture retracts frankincense according to schedule. Seizures recur at a driven pace distinct from pacem. Daily bratwurst generates angular bread, whose vendor will remain a geometric whiz. One crawls to his stall awaiting battle or a strict new prize.

Brahman protects candor but cancelled flights vowel the brain into fatal error blue. Up without down splits hairs for a C- in mathematic wonk. Frantic cartoon charms yeast's gab chatter solid as pages mourn decisive blows to claim the Heisman curse in bursts.

Candor bleaches mathematics, unless age-old prophecies harm the rain. One error or two? The uptown mimicry of sage behests repeal all wonking. Any Heisman lurch will undo hat tricks passing as acclaim. Each time yeast is mentioned, there's a down vest.

Downdraft shylock of hi-lo *que es* erratic unsavory night flier. This o'clock works so let's teach a habit. Air clothesline mechanics of wind on deliverance terms. Ice the club room boasting unashamed how with onlooker relief entrenched in symbol she lives in hiding.

Hives mask hurt. That is specific. Very antsy terms clock fortified. New loomed pulp. Pumice shapes the host. A halo ratchets up bombastics in another sphere. An embolism very *not yours* makes me tremble anyway. She thrives. I keep the lid on usually tight.

Bluster is just that. Endemic to her. Extant ant hill, big pharma festina transpiring a lump detected because someone is missing where they promised solicitation, ear to earache. Lounges amass in the bends. Her listening tightens the tremor. I do so I may forget.

Miss breath's licit torque. Amendments miss the integral amassing of vented spleen. Spiral energy decants the will. A missive draws in promised take. The ventricles appear in weeds and summer full of trills relaxes body from its rounds of lift and shallow fall.

Hyperion is a tussle of miscues, gaseous trifecta alloyed, propped upon the point of entry: fossil. Somber for descant spillway, *contrare* speed on subway platform where your mantis negates another's head. 'Tis the 'tis which shortens the breath of stealth.

Way too mythocentrist form is. Spatulae do more than gather; they alloy plats. Do you remember where we put the fossil? Wreath on wreath of steal-good mesmery inflates the faultline where indecent pass-throughs overdose our rigor as though *de rigeur.*

If it scampers, fork over the stable degree. Stay truthful to increment, myelin-ated, in vitro. Unpleasantry drives the bare, offhanded miter. Craving scores on Varilux for flashback. Every border takes an oath of office. Pink overbooks the pimento's motif, framing it.

~

Cremation's just this. Booking and modality, a fragment back to north. The mitt was full of leather speed. Overtly showing in the wake of an announcer's feed (and the reverse). A verse goes to sure thing, official, yes, and counting. Driven (never) to despair, unless...

we testify. Broken into words against the advice of chirping. How happy hour will matter less than speeding off, abort abort: the past proxy of fear. She'll be back in the swing catatonic, her rhyme. Standing there, needing reassurance under the hood, *welcome to*

homogenized charisma. All the Jelly Belly bowls evoke a *wing-it* attitude, bug-in-your-ear emoticons, and silt. The test of handing off is whether any crash tones spark some accolades. And if a dapper fellow in the third row should begin to vocalize in thirds,

squeamish eighths will bind you to Bailey's falsified effects, nog on the sleeve, ties tight en loco parentis *gutentag pobrecito*— to avoid convoy's wrong turn at the well, bolstered by prolific pursuit of mosquito-born dim sum where bells crack morbidly to appear clearer

although nearer to the boisterous heart, the half sweet rack and pinion grinds out lineation, one urn at a time, *poquito* obvious as promotional piece(s) perched atop svelte saplings showing yogic moves each once in a while, the anticipated effects of clairvoy's sutra market stacked up against octagon's rowdy curriculum of aussie indie trash FYI an electorate impaired. Life-threatening tip tap foot-in-mouth game on colada overflow blacklists the hunt & peck LOL (on ignore) a shepherd's day approved for consumptive

loud crickets scheduled to implode will also wild on sched- if pina c. is minced inside the heck-of-it, *mark my word*. whose hindrance is a comely shepherd with the sum up sleeves of which we've never heard. instinct remains a short story, thrashing to get out?

Rooibos finds its citric gloss in time. Tangiers as panacea to the –rine. Diced beside feckless Q: balding, amorous as Goering. Flint prowls the station major. A series swept. Get blue, pay later. Refused wor(l)d doorways a heave-ho. Cathects the hoax it bows to.

Red is bountiful. Minor pacts reuse their aldermen. Memento tat when trade-shows scat sing rouge darling lieder. Craft's a toddy and we have the light to show. A moment of the wept enforcement pours across time at the pace of a swift door kick. Cataract's a guess.

Won't color come to commercial inroads, lock horns, halt the cornerstone après le bain hose down tempo, bare a morsel, debunk Adam's folly? Foreground tips itself toward the foaming chrysalis, circle weeps a hole-in-one. Wall squares off to discredit who did what.

Remember bunk is tooled from scratch. Hole-in-the-wall has learned to rhyme with hole-in-one. The squires shift in their easy chairs while peasants weep for credit. Corners on the market gradually equate to inroads sans dead ends. The tipping point's an alter ego.

December slumps apple-a-day G-force globes "light it up" for deadline the answer flows, opprobrium? Not really. Así, así. Regift that clashing sigh, steel to bone's grafted sighting. Planetary sip says why not please her so the wick may sleep unguarded there.

Intermittent body armor might displace a sigh. *Are you aware, or under there?* The ceiling slights the rug. Here we go again. The guards are angry. Dogs are bright. Lashing equals weeping gnashing teeth point three to five. A lump a day's the same as no outlet, whiter than a blaze. Wile E. strip searches top to bottom the s-word sale: Here shrouded eggs winter well. See it as the slick repeat repeat / rest. The third shooter half cocked a bit too close for wet lashes, outstretched, drags his boyish quarrels out front.

Developing cellblocks mountain up the salt lick. Best to leave that out of the equation. Half the crop dust maintains office hours in drag. The querulous notary prompts hoots of recognition. Run that by me again. Trip lurch hastens gravity, all hale and arty

barkeep targets concierge critique. The guest-go-round is a warden in question mark data mine. Energy is cramped muscle frilly boa the I love madlib smack-down prude land jamming him at the line. On the run, artsy lam trips the haystack node, submits

rude inference held to (the vest) chested ostracist libation-prone and larky on the brink of ark and indigo beneathings. Unlaminated rippage stacks the trek from here to mittenburg where wardens troll the gentry lake with amperage to baste and mangle off-shore.

Nonlocal musing yokes sand to breast to xylophonic yes, frigidly buffeted and snarky these allegiances re- re- re- (quire) as they form. Forsaken to contrive chute and ladder amp'd extrastellar episode. Woolen craft, mark your spartan skins with iron-on plymouth.

Stellographers in bulk arrived at the expensive craft to mark their spartan chalkings. Forsaken averages induce the view of a squire's side. Hues along the wool face shake out episodes from strangers who inform the local with their dust. Sans traction, anyone

quibbles and represses, but when you were a girl / when you were a boy he examined a timing device priority junk mail harassment sacking York the quicksilver if I may be so bold as to misgreet you raising eyebrows to Arbus and her declaration of beaux-arts.

Are you seeing double, D? Those twins lack verve. We're pained in scope diving for deutschmarks at mid-cent- capsized anklets on our rims to mine the pressing quicksand normed to paint a brow some color of the row. In coiled neglect one sets priorities, one ropes off the cherry farm and gerrymanders its frogs so they answer to a higher plague click into bra strap paper clip, a turn of phrase six pence and three euros as plot-sprint otherwise called *near future*. Gag gag agh is accomplice droplet parting fact from detail's

regalia (full to roaring) bratwurst lip print armed in daguerreotype across from pentecostal merriment the rocks and art formations seeming Euro-paeans tracked by natural gag orders typed in futura, slapped on urns all six of them to swerve the depths

where tattoos flower in Cannes bailing out ailing rye with a traceable rivet (zinfandel). Doggerel leaps onto climbers extrapolated from ice pocket eucharist at ten past noon – weary of road rules speared as they struggle for the cockpit, podium taking on milky

war tunes creped across arugula with peeled notoriety might crush the zen in triplicate before copies are made. A peer review pits clock against format, and limbs go limber any old conveyor belt where dim sum rests. The ribald tracing arm needs zin to go

propagating down the outbound wire, instead installs the update twixt firm ament to cap stegner flunkies, bake and shake the obseq- stop ream, fleer wiki entry or topsoil whip (pony's depakote quirk), but don't compose yourself outside a grunt at the streampoint.

Tall dates mend the lunkheads who might make a wiki out of whipstitch quirks. But that's another stunt we'll leave to depakote. Imposing sides on circles is a flee-brained trick. How about downing kefir at a gulp? It will sustain your meantime as the town goes silk.

Add the lactobacillus so she can distill the funk of perfect sleepers, whine *oh not again* if cracked tibia black label warning should bellyflop into square's abandoned kiosk rip-off. Noncommittal task of PTA implosion lures itself into submission, skinsurf blathering on.

Who had the sunscreen last? The only cure for passive aggressive quaintlings is dark visors pulled down around the lobes. Flopped disks belly up to baro-metric prestidigitation in a tiff and time lag commits faux pas on the surf of it, post lather and post pondering.

Is Saturn owned? SPF, the formulary. We insects, bodhisattvas, scaled down to nubs syntactic lipstick— laser / goggles / premonition disavows discus silvers in transit laze over Technotitlan, skanked latex of time's churlish technical glow as botanical distance.

Formarian contrasts snip vows after disco bot clucks skankily, behind goggles googling dis-fests slivery and lazily with sections perfected to the nubbins (nine) of which bods have their lariats affixed to bull, the driven Saturns, sticking to the Jupiterial protectorate.

Chariot for dimpled grub, the Taurus reclusive grabs at fast track for mylar's aging snipe. Riverview surplus, anti-scent of amputated lanyard. Fake it, okay? Where we signify halo, a saki perspiration. Mercury spells its strong-armed steering column demonology.

As for the Sag-, a lanyard won't support sporadic space subsumed into the – scopic geometric whatsit maybe fake and maybe simply spirited. Tracking devices devised for nagging backstroke nab what perspicacity is left post-aspiration in a wink these hours.

Worry blooms in fair territory. Stove of delta. Rule or ritual. Amarna, *a double please*. If only the sadhus bend the arrow, a whatchamacallit (next to no one) I am / parcel as epoxy gone fishing all the while you are somewhat alive, god forbid they turn back.

Riches harmed by pox on houses proxy depth perception. Closed-captioned Alamogordo reaps what thou hath sown. Bid me *adieu,* said they. No next a bout face prints on the binding propped up north. The looms are fairy dust profuse with seeping.

South's underwater note procreates person-to-person or P2P as raised treasure of I am awakening— condemned kiss. Is impugned, castle. On squirrel's memory such is bliss filled pawprint in *carpe* unlike any accuser *diem* sprays the cabinets with psychotropic.

Quarrels dim bliss, the carping's all pugnacious and mnemonics do not help. The kelp still rattles fourth-stage cussed craft unless the not-willing reassurance implicates the praline-prone low-wit waterlogged accusation-prone one-sided choir tilted to the right.

I won't fight / this / that / the other. Introducing "-" in the NW corner wearing the hula skirt of lightweight pause, pinecone life striates Monday morning front page (retrospectively) *is this your card?* No one's voice rings true at the choral quenching of it.

Tinctures of evocation glint upon the weight of cones imbued with pagination. Is the rule a thumb print? Very savvy pauses speak resplendency. A brother redefines a corner full of space. The light is everywhere he sings. I hear his beachfront halo matching lace.

One among Bermudian they in kind dazzle with atheistic energies. A clearing coats. So-so minnows whose fins allay drift-ing, patched with indices and *good speed, sir* you rummage through memorabilia: bi-relational spoonlit parallels, return address backhoe.

Spectacles gather memorial species, parching once dictation's spooled from generation. Dawn to dashing magi, the Bermuda fling is razz material, theistic and yet plain. The clear young knowns obtain empirical fin-toned bicyclical omens to increase one's reach.

Speech heckles the speaker, rolls its epitome out, flaxen rec stop pause ff rw. Tutorial orange crush where I must duck to find the favor. Whizzing speck I want to break free from the sartorial spacecraft audit. Be vaccinated against within-reach snoozing birth.

His rush of craft birth immersed onlookers in a tome with rolled "r's" netting peak pro forma tattered with material one wades in before drying, the equivalent of forgetting match points. Auditory remnants teach the mood to lift within the reach of parallels.

Missing form. Just yet. A throng in my adenoids if I could only have memorized what you became before you attained (saved by) aegis, the rousing conversation of ex-pat flame retardant noises babble in dried waves and impoverished goings-on.

Wrong deciduous formations qua memoranda. Foreground savvy versed in lame rabble point of view. Tenacity's a glib endorsement of routine. Singing stays reserved (for days) like this: replay. Repeated choice turns verbs to parchment at the dawn of pretty noise.

Alias travels on a tight schedule, said shed-wool. Plan C builds case sensitivity straight up blind as. Shale climbs the northern face. Ozone, sure of itself. Speak or be reduced. Ask: *can't a person be QUIET*. Well, sure. The figure-ground (-) tridactyl hangs in there.

Plan R tacks the quill pen diatribes to new semesters languishing in duct tape swirls as if the ace anticipated were deformed in light. The woo-woo factor trills a wooden flute tune behind a veil of capstoned tailgate smarty-pants as lasses fight to clear the trail of foam.

To the nines. Brecht's sugar mill. A vulture of lectureship. Voltage, yes. Er, how-would-it. Appear. Side by side, siamese tote bag flush. Full house against a fermi, dealt fairly across ectopic channels. Tower she pinned her hair back by, fooling the typecast cantor.

Culture quacks a little to the left of closure striving toward the status of unpinned. One casts for incantation, lush green etcetera brought mill-ward, true, and sapped. The levitation sides with treading water on the periodic table, housed within the lab(oratory).

Braying, one dies before learning to, I guess, touch toes. Isn't it subtle, much the way marriages happen, then unhappen, how if a symbol rejects itself, euro sign pound sign evacuates the punctilious "do all that," frustrating centennial islet as day shrinks.

Earning traps touched toes. Sub-par rages perhaps symbolize the round cents one divulges if at all. The rust set into daylight pounds out die-cut ounces of flesh lacking acuity until the hap-net bulges with surrender. Then is mulch a way of growing in.

I am sand before the premise of motion, sorely missed, to grow older out of sensible portion, round as we seem. Lust for the as-is. No returns, exchanges. Well, dreams maybe, go blank before someone notices, checks the pressure and level, stands still.

Regression to the mean connotes as-ism pressureless state of being, having been tilled and then rectified beyond the walled demise of a motet. In church, the movements leap from staves, and sent rice splayed into the air portends a joining that will last, and . . .

(the longest non-stop break rhapsodizes) crass dust flattened. This will change your meager involution. Huddle up, hangman militant, third child of nowhere. Collar the e pluribus "we will vigorously forget" as group home adds another bride fasts *I lost her*

Match point severs the agronomy. Does one condone what breaks (the land)? In thirds the ratcheting comes silver. Blanch. A rigor spots long pauses, seeking to contextualize. One collars home and eases out a voluntary *non-* as if to whisper and receive.

Caesura quality first a full-figured crop circle. Main course is doleful, lower than fif ti eth breast of flushed hatchet art. See you can't divide zero, but bear the brunt of our con tin uity of butterfly ratios / or quivers, easy does it. *Blech*, a compliment to . . . oh, goodness.

Queasy butterflies subtract from complement of the x axis of a breathful earth. What continuo affords the quiver easing static dole. Without caesura, figures drop. The art of leaving well becomes enough alone time for zero bases to come forth, not hither.

Killjoy stock footage should know better than to solicit agency's input, or mixology IF illogical pass / fail aeronautics succeeds where y-z dubs the hearth (embassy of synth triple hop) digit: a one-bedroom one-bath caveat emptor farming out its baseline strata.

Patchwork quill pen tempts arm-besting to a one-room anathema. A dub detector dis-enfranking -ologism ails the pool, the weak, while insincere bass plagiarists triplicate a prior logic vetted by the king quintet that runs the farm as an illicit agency prevaricates.

Lies? By a hair, many are worse off, isn't that a variant. Yo is missing u (turn) boxer refreshes to beat the monoxide turf whistle broadsiding new fall collection satire of el niño duplicate, beheading "six underground" to encourage rubber stamp departure.

Nets gather up *los niños* histogrammatically faulting no lecturer who tires of replication. One's favorite intellect recalls a comment on the cloddish rubber stamp as all moved through the customs line. *All thumbs*, said he. His entourage a kind of small collection.

Queued, stoked, drowsy, fists ready, but slack . . . relaxed there, laid back, One Reality. For diazepam, a signed waiver, savior and witness. Rattler, sound of maracas, cap-click gently neglects samba, passage. Ha, Ellis *who*? She survives us, bare skin and all.

Let the witness respond to sonorous cha cha, sipping tea with kin, the at-bliss specter of condoning zeal intently waiting for a savior. Laxity's the signed is-net, porous with reliance on a laid-bare head apart from a mantilla corresponding to the nearest prayer.

Whatever chooses this, dances to stand back. From lookout night, incoming night, all is woeful chatter. Dial-a-date fends off dropped calls so earth comes down on you. The incurable condition of people, or wo (men) romancing reason— partly— ever.

Sever the rein-donned premises from being on the look. Flight comes in. Watch tempered glass. The overtones breastfeed luminary voyages toward *here*. Relate. Inflate remove the late cures from each chosen. No one looks askance at primitive delays.

A pavilion is not enough for subservient flight. Heaven, thickly ravened, preboards. "The wheel" a play on nothing bears a proper subtext for supper, expunges love's schlepped quantum, the redundant *if-and* excreting simplified ways we spoon closer.

Venn diagrams depict a thing in things in things. Context's upper hand seems altogether pungent, and why not? The simple truth is pontoon boats are crafted with a slip of crazy underneath. Ears give good glow to ravenous being. Enough so that a violin is rained on.

Confetti dejects a person. Celebrity dreams, what they seek from you. At least from themselves. Go to this source, that hinge. Apply for withdrawal. Be denied twice, three times. A room listening to its own standstill is not a room plagued with emptiness.

Inflections breed less certain text. A binge of listening inverts itself. Emptiness makes the room. Denial frosts the source. If words could plaster structure, they would seek from you themselves. Defection has to mean procession in measures of one. Withdrawn.

Rarely, if ever. Oh is O. Sorry for that, I guess. One-upmanship drops a vapor, a hint bends your majestic let-down, counters *do unto* ice shelves scowling from the last row. *Dearly departed we gather* boutique's chichi reconnaissance replies, nose up, defiant.

They had a row, defying present tense. A mint version of pleasure pores over the drop kick blade of envy. Sorrow hastens backlist countdown until each one would rather know a ploy for giving guesswork its full due. Ice lit majesty unties reminders of the rendering.

Ungainly fissure, what keeps changing. Peel is a new emollient of ginger. Ask if she's yielding yet or whether lactose is worth the kneel-down prefab haggada, purified topic swatting at your astonished lull in thought, groves bookended by three liters of truce.

Change makes lakes into white bookends. Wait! The task in urgency amounts to lactose-free toned images come to a lull in half-time ruse. The mole between our walls wields debt offensive so the take is full, and not this mini-liter of lab coat clothing.

Rinse the calypso rockface. Delicate woman as compadre, her rose fad delinquent elevation found concocting some woozy parable, chalking ceilings for ease. Upset Avogadro's purse, the ask-now-pay-later with its cadre roaring, a yew tree beautified.

Levitation leaves the woose from turning chalk. Believe the upset payback to have been delivered in Morse Code. Who's responsible for the CAD system gnarled and patterned? Padres leave beatitudes in a shambles. Facing the wound like men unfurled thanks-free.

Packed full of superfluous scrub and cover. Trinity wishes you in, trickles down. Pristine nominee. Screen gazer. To the computer-aided southwest span, in half. Connects dots anomie shouldn't be looking after, except that it does. Accredited destiny asks no favors.

Rub a drubbing and then pine before the favored species all at once full of the West spanning a million psyches. Gazing out the screen's path, the tines appear to scope out less than half the creed. Playthings are always fractions covering the exceptional look.

When turning a page, chez soi contracts. Spelunking to The Baths, brother is noetic, concept-prone. Survival rates right up there with you-know-who, but at home his love of transfat build-up opens irrelevant pores, serving them to the writ of life expectancy.

Silken honeybees revert to soldiering. Elapsed love rates with page flight. Ore contains, while home navigates vivacity held at the bottom of the pond. Wrath holds still while rights give ground. Activitat's wholly immersed in transcendental waivers. Here is fate.

Such is news. I didn't intend to estrange buds "where the heart is" attenuated, wilts mining a vital ray, *hop to it*, perspicacious and backpedaling travels with misfortune. Care for it, no matter how lucky. Irrigate the spore of twilight a cheek transfers there.

Heart goes strong versus heart falls back. Hers grew larger than one knew, despite inevitable expectations. Hops did damage. Pedaling stayed vast. The here is rarely fully now. To wit, the clarity may revel in remote transfiguration, pending pluck and twilight.

Light of twos, pairings save the renovation, every spoke a terrace rife with straw. Cold fingers aggrieve the flame. Pastime panics the honeysuckle. Neck impassible, this lorry of wooden breath, a staircase buttoned to the throat attracts a sanguine match.

Hatched tonnage holds to grounded past. The heck of it hisses raw, old pacts. As if enlisting were the same as wooing. Non-two tones amounts to oats. The passage of spokes steeling down divided high(ways). Meantime inno-renno-vatio races with life.

Laws of snowflake blue into grace-gray, pepper the chain of command with tastes open formal inquiries into leisure, smack of over-thinking, call it desertion, how many shoulders wake up motorists, clog appetites, rumble: *shhh, the green apparel of cause.*

Quirks in weather story our lives, ease furs winter once inside, the scenes, replete with many forms of rum leading to rumination. Appetites grow long as green mid-pasture in another time. The motor grace becomes stays steady as the knitted chain with haste.

Flash fire heralds Ouroboros when operant SoCo (my way) is renounced, edges the pile forward, a family convenes, soused. So much for hand raising the root word: Cadmus, Aquitaine, Apollo real to the wind. No, since we might authenticate the link with story . . .

Narrativity shakes off polling place, thereby our betting tendency. To trust or to employ discernment. To discern versus allow in wind. Tick tick tick and hinges herald the oncoming weather that displays the operative who-done-it, perhaps a moot point.

Native volunteer: captive. I am, or else. I say. Gamble a people. Creeks: a terminology. Holophrastic dents glower at the gallery crowd, prance-iple (stipulation?) the loving look disparages mom/pop: trim emphasis on who the unexplained departs from— normalcy.

Hook points shift the daylights out of else. Popular lore has gales of trees remotely limber in a dizzy wind. Phases of the hologram infract the pores of pull. Replace each one with rowdy lightning and prepare to liberate the lacings. Frightening tents now freed.

The gift is an inherited illusion. Lair resists folk remedy. Very touchy, *tsk* the roughshod fraternal bond leaves home at night. A pioneer's portrait endures the full spa treatment prophylaxis, a directory of mutual libations. Nails anchoring an outdoor venue come free.

Air's duration rectifies a failure to liberate. Ratios of anchor lull the crew to sleep, while being shod beneath the eaves. Elusive thinking stills the home pact constantly remedial while laxity results in folk tunes where the classics might have been, a reified tall praline.

I may not last long as a paragon of whatever is just so. Calcite will end the registrar's function. I've got your calyx "cut bait" limewire (lackluster kiss) right here. What good are pacification drills if the line snaps, the crime of it recommitted, drained from blond chi?

Tar's a feather of its own. The late wire misses nap songs. Cognizance stiffens up against the chi relayed by other sources. Lime dustings coat the through way, just as oregano redeems pacific wheat. So long as functions craft these rills, we'll sleeve spice lessons in stick-to-it-ness, amortizing the nursery vibe. Darjeeling admits a least squares ethic. Starch dangles less precious baggage, its *do not cling* gardening motto, a paunch of barley on one end of the scale tipped, emboldened

with tipped change from monastic sacrifice that lingers as a vibraphone opposing mittens at an angle near the snow thistled on end with starch no longer precious, rather angular as distinct from a square pragma. Known long continents arrest these nesting instinct,

winnowing thought invests colt's tame delivery with autographed alms piously spaced, a mixed bag precip— no explanation. Tirade's eye and populist report gashes the crate for time, unspecified incitements and elsewhere that frost-bitten bird slashing shoreward

else a rating planes across the *am* shouldering graphic piety. Aiding and abetting chapters not yet hatched, while tines prick specks mottled and in thirds played to unnamed shores vested in autodidact prescience. Chain gangs virtually delimit pronouns

today, tonight, tomorrow. Net worth recoups tuition. Monistic defeat is deafness. Bibliotheca forgets age and weight, cashes in on vacation negatives, centerfolds cleansed with absinthial glitter. Asphyxiant pledge burns its only bridge after sentencing climaxes.

Replenished weight is how to think, not how to come down, bridging excess with lenses that no longer fit. Cinch is how the next breath will be seen. The earning power of sentences will max out monody, or nimble weather figures into an eternity of equation.

Threnody adds a pound per metacrisis even though bodywork shows exceptional rapport. A factotum among downers, heads are caught subbing for eclectic size. Eleven histories uncollapse the genial excerpt. Case in point reinvents the In/Out diorama.

2.

Sublet fate for a limited time. It was an honest mistake, the extra cocktail. Don't breathe, but let it be confidant; we'll grow to enjoy leeway as only blond canaries pluperfect as finch and grosbeak paradox glow painted redaction leans on pump alleviating prime numbers. How is it three becomes a whittled tent on loan, and whose idea was it to deliver propane accent with the baked goods? Posture frames prime festival against the greed. Any throwaway faith ought to be divided equally among the parsnip cooks deploying soon. What's more, the white caps one associates with self-cleansing alarm become synonymous with *else*. No matter how configured purity might seem, there always has been clay, and there are pores from which to draw. This moment in particular relieves the past of obligations to seem multiple. Our crisis, after all, is lived one syllable at a time, within the confines of two-four time, while tithing.

Get, capture, process, build. Stone shelves lift twelve openings. Toned selves minufecture closet space apace. Finding the cage door splintered open, predestination shakes hummingbirds from throat or furnace or exhaustion. Blimps hold still, at least to the imagined eyesight. Frames wound contents. Form cures content. Ruminary crevices detach the length from legroom. The prefect has to dance a minuet alone. To own what is pre-owned. Like curvature, the protean replacement of water. Churning. Hurtful wheels synonymous with stasis half persuasive yawl. A hub forms around watching. Splotches of gray paint change even the inner room. Nachos no longer sustenance address some whims aside from whimsy. The child knows nothing important will ever be counted, but why? If binoculars spread their double negatives like fictions. . . If they crush a heaven whose knife is left out on purpose . . . body will blurt out facts, figures, reduce the rod and cone count by thirty, encourage listening devices to arrest, book, and judge the encounter.

Whose single negative is stripped like parasitic car part swapped for permit? Belles run yonder in the crash course bleeding. Blend run torques the seed field. Tended test scores boil the pot. Who is clocking algebra performed in half tense collar points? Called upon relenting premises too many chefs. If pressure is a premise, what is haze about to do apart from strangling plans? Who will adjudicate missing ingredients (paprika, sage) for speed (lounge music) and convenience? Noblesse oblige means ocean's glacier expands its reference list to include the endangered. Specious arguments tempt teething and later in the evening, desiccated as roots. Every three hundred years, meaning accretes a habit: mess kits, turntables, somatic rhythms trashed for their giving nature. Churn, *demand*, sleep poorly on stakes.

Cautionary torment sprawls upon oulipo recount, tale of the tape. If anybody wants to call out the familiar integer equating this person, do so now. Naturally occurring sentences afford a bleak array of stuttering to spec. Supremacy insists upon itself. Alternatively a curled hub gives cults grasp of any tabled brass. A host is personified, though rarely interfered with. Violence and sherry occur unsheathed in tandem. Text messages forgo the eyes and smile to hide skirt length, take for instance norms among starlit weeds. And stricture. And a siege to come of African daisies, a posh Rosetta in the median. And cameras, lodestones that persist in carrying the bad with the half-good superlatives in one backpack.

Him (objecting): I followed the orders to amuse waterpark out of tourist rush, but it happened much slower than you might have expected. I don't know what you *must* like, or are forced to like; however, I know how I lose myself.

Her (transitively): Let go your mirror before it makes us aware of what we are doing. Are we similar again? Against my better justice? *No longer do I think alone.*

Manned faucets leave exchanges trades to fund paprika assembled in a nether hook line's synchronous nefarity. Obsessive compass meant to travel. Octopus disrestrictions. Paint this wisecrack north. So forth sewn on. Cross stitch minus semaphore addresses only heartache, when the problem forms new consciousness. *I used to list with you.* Come here already and gloss ingredients with me, come swim to selves, trim the mature rods from sterling confined to spring collection. Infancy's the cusp of senior status. He might have indulged himself. I have on tape the mention. Possibly, where light bends back on itself, pronouns can be more than they are tilted to be, while the betrothal coats three yellows found in our syllabic paint shop library. Patronymic volleys leave a child pre-scorned. Once caged, the humming starts to sound like unions lying in state.

A thin slice. Let me restate. Aplomb.

Nordic thing means half your exercise amounts to purest zilch.
Ascorbic ping. Time-out.
A frenzy is not equal
To a friend. Hard of incredible (-dulous) feeling.
Shut up. Authoritative, precious.

Him: Excuse classification from class or skylark, dismal purpose— whichever.
Her: Ice used to be a parity prod-. Now thinking confiscates such winces . . .
(butterfly my depth)

Suspicion heavy sentiments leave outer skin as cold as absent, unattended and
qualified as breath. Is it the victim's afterthought or a professional courtesy?
My land is seared by craft kicks. Who has curiosity: the bully under pressure,
or the most recent victim? We are undressed for no apparent pleasure. In the
kitchen eggs are syllables. Being prepared, shaped into rational silence. Brass
tosses its badges and teases the pot calling— forget black. Go ahead and
practice being the naysayer harvesting sponge proceeds going to patch
dysfunction and hyped score. The core gradation of selections from the
periodic table match her gaze to heaven after razing solemn place. What you
want is a pompadour to pull over your near-death attitude. Commence in due
course to want something considered extant. A mercenary strategy includes
outlined stretch pant chalk markings, how we remove journal entry from
incident, the days that remain.

No one: are you leery of presence? Pretext? Patronize the nimble confiscation of
interiors no one has known?

Plus two: children resolve their power loss

Should that have been married? Enough guessing, it *is* wed to motive. Only
you can prevent a suit while they suture decrepitude to the dissident clue.
What seemed thought-out has been carved into a vested plan. There's one
questionable intent bargain hunting versus shopping digging *um* out of—
second hand answers. Bolts are bolts. And stew enables *rue the day*. Torsion's
flippant. A camisole's mimetic body pratfall oversees the call person-to-person.
Catch me doing something taut. Tautology is boy-girl as it relates to the
previous brass knocked off its pageant. If you're of my ilk, you can beat me to
your repartee. Bodiless and spare and wasted. "I have scuffed the lotus."

Torque's not usually bottled (up). Cement the part that is not ship-shape. Stuck
in someone's blogocratic napalm Sencha canister.

Well then, all right. Why don't we handle this *in*-house. The bugged deception
finishes its thought before commissioning mown silk.

Milky little ways through north might mean that Gladstone (to the left) is
reeling (still). The doe kneels. Upheaval signals for mercy.

Meet you at the tantrum tousled outhouse revived with paint. Vivace is the movement we've been waiting for. Trailers where they load stretchers between the brother walls. A bag of trash. A bagged stone wall, catching up with bygones for caustic kickbacks. I'll give you a good deal if you'll fill me in on filming neighbors who try to be friends in name, address, number. Parrots run giddy on filched seeds. The circuit crimsons its way into habitude. Unless you want to be divine, stay in one piece and jump ahead of circumstance, if only to bleed on white sheets dreamed then made host system. Intrinsicity might offer sprockets one can track. And that's not all: fervor is your very own to keep.

Lone zones martyr us. (revise) Lone fields run deeper than your diary. (revise) Lone pronounces taint with shaken shoulder as if emphasizing how the petered-out *in principio* might mean the end of learning (curve).

He spouts spont- and now look.
            aneous   and sharp

A simile shortens its overnight stay by order of maximum height. *Are you as tall as waste dumps in the east? She pointed me there to say that people who have died are all hers.* Can you fathom a worm-eaten Messier A, the story line? Her only symptom of a story was the probability of its being hocked for a hold symbol. Streams line the moon, Ptolemy first and Alphonsus after twin rupes, scarps cut short the ejecta. Listen to my opening line: a fella went to see the lockdown master and was begging for his strife, the only way he knew. Next thing, a raven flew into the capillaries, as if (who knew) A blue tint stayed residual in a stray home. The stray, knockoff of the red bloom. Despite the lampoon, carnivals preempt a likely dowry. Dowel of hippocampus, fitful as seventh place stuck in drive (D4). Meet you in the langlab. Strut first forthwith. The instructor demonstrates fetal position; cloud and firmament memorize the entire coda. The zenith has a short "e" sound out of his mouth as fresh as daisy wheel. Brother against brother, eighties where they waver. Watch me, Mom. Watch. Mom: *watch!* Being— in a proper, capitulated sense. Health or prana mascot we-care-a-lot industry loses pitch. Perfect your noose for me alone. Industrious new mood forms feast lines feline famine *wunst*. Coordinating conjunctions latch onto key lime conduct, pie for later. You should have nicer acquaintances between your faith and résumé. Are you altogether obvious when you denote? You can quote those who are tested, tried, bored by booming voice. Beginning regresses one azure at a time. III. without II. or I. squibs the hardened exemplar as deviant designee. Sister pitted against mother, son against sister. If I practice crying, do you promise you can wilt me? Speak not of ability, but of solemn preference. You can imagine how water is the most partial element. Organically certified perjury peters out; soon they're all caught broadcasting from the before/after dais.

Ability is not the same as prejudice or purging.
Repeat (tough to be ignored) after me: *Silence is no gift until you mean it.*
    Excalibrate yourself. Totter.

Chemical fire proviso domesticates company pups. Lumpen dichotomies invest in sugar beets. Revive me while I'm young. Stillborn (as distinct from synecdoche) reverie encompasses sine waves trained on you. Repeat zones inhale/absorb/derail the op cit litmus breast. Companion peaceable's impeccable *please*. Please pass . . . Overseas, best behavior grows visually dense while weekend visitors tangle on the grand staircase, a choice between Caribbean stud, Let It Ride, and three-card feedback lunge. For placebo's sake, brothers who never argue over intelligent origins fall back to sleep. I'm timing you now in your indebtedness. Let's design a no-nonsense kama sutra to mop up the enumerated blow. *If you were stranded. If* the lighthouse were delusion, dilettante siren (lacking) leitmotif, if swollen passages gave graft its due, if sentences were few—

List of last resort

Rutabaga, corn meal, Yukon gold, distilled white vinegar, pseudoephedrine, pop quizzical mantra, dim chakra, point-five, limberlost once limber, cauterized stroganoff, climb out of the dungeon précis, jump ball, steins of water, fresh zed, blancmange, serenity, forecast frocks, Opici splits, tasseled fromage, creosote mouthwash, triple bock, full court press, tsetse fly lipid

(this is goodbye then mano-a-mano?)

Infinite flaw is a choice   doesn't waffle Once up
our most trying face time Wazzup is administered
fleeing's easy Once upon a flub
Craft tupper(night)mares your mildest inch itches (don't reach
scratch apply liberally) Stand up sit down state of the
North slurping its last-stand Feast rightuptotheballdrop rup
ture tour's Gone with glup

During your last trip a week ago, you rehearsed or circulated a new release, *so thus* let's begin with *In the beginning there was a word* the crossterm eminent domain cosmetics at cloud's disfigurement, whereby we paid a surcharge to sign in or out and dot the i. Domus dominis paternum [independent of] monogamy where it commenced— paper or plastic. Jaunt is my one venture into color wheel, said the intelligible coarse replica of maiden caste. Froth's my middle name. Conform to pieces. Then we'll vote. On voyage and in tote

dismemberment

(monastic gid)

      ii. headpiece question playing for keeps (thought used once runs deep with meadow foxes), discontent as the best scenario, nine were welcomed in, two excluded, one managed to slip past the dogs, a shame about the warbler, the dodo, the solitaire, the Great Auk, the loss of candor
                        etc. the excitable
content-rich revenue cart straps
child seat plastic coating may suffocate
egg gatherers who approach the
Labrador Duck perspiring

All she wants to do is fracture moods I thought were mine.

(transform the haricot vert   the wave   abbreviated choking you call   mp3 instant)

Phonetic photogrip, don't forget that a visible interjection may cause gripes to be rubbed down. Have you seen the rubbing alcohol wedged into the motet? This does not include "righteousness" nowadays in quotations as we lie down or don't lay anything down since that is the wrong way of organizing the science of minimum wages. There's one who is wise, perseverating on nothing. Chasmic lintel, spent lens denigracias might harm the wrestled spacetet to the flauta while we single out the hungry.

Give me back my flurry, said the cheese.

Cakewalk clobbers set piece, no? A sober ceiling, the mounting munition, she sleeps with him, he sleeps with her.

Sobriety's a kind of curve ball.

Fulsome, isn't it here, where the novella ash tiptoes down from half-inch below the waistline or knuckle. It's getting difficult to see . . . fire too low for the nola,

your highness, here to report everyone who misconstrues a definition as in
faux resplendency, when it has been amended tenderly, as though the wok
with "tendre croppes" lies down to pale oil and mutiny.

Final reminder. You won't receive the 72 names for the group piloted by astro-
epic feat invasive vita widely known as "the other" *one* not *two* zuzim, so
please without regard for limbs, pick up Oxford dress shirts and landmark the
boarded-up tug whose seer is on long-term disability and could return at any
suitable break in the slide show mimicry, unprotected as finestra. Button down
the notary and try to spice a different date. Notice a sharp jug of fragments to
your left, don't touch anything, put the raft on your back and topple the
coliseum you're plainly darting to (get in line) the next phase, your haute
spiffed couture less like modal womb.

Compared to *what*, he asked?

I may not be the best at anything   that, as they say, is that
He is my everything   liquidity of what I ought to be, left home
I am happy just to know that I'm his child   we'll see about a hearse

His charity lumbers through the tall dark trees of torsion lucid once now dour

Pasteurized, centered on the page, approximately whitened, fur and fir and
forthright.

A wild ride is how he
characterized my having known
the other

                              gold in the shadow (on rafters, too)
                              flecks me   suspends
                              conceives   stalemate   peek-a-

Sprawl may levitate for purposes of match
point

                        source consorts
                        with birthplace Once we were
                        two lanes, in fact, closed (to wit)

cane sugar easily translated into sucre bounces
            day of emergence (timbre willing)

        one is not
        meant to emigrate (Briggs Type Indicator)

I am this, *and you are?*
(waiting to pick up my Oscar, ma'am.)

Also: (*spirited* does not show by itself)
furniture allegedly won't hold
value   when brads of atmosphere slide
                         into place
also
when the block put in to hold the car in park
had been released
                         I put out my hand just like you said
the vehicle sped in reverse
right into the retaining wall
                         watch that truck   the deep
                         will want to claim you
and as a child he
concluded
something from

                endings

                    belted mass
                    how can I
                    get in there   desire the versatile

mirror   open its fires
(mid-range) penathol drip
in retrospect   drab   a hundred thousand

                             extra moldings   "lone wolf"
                             seltzer cooler talk mercury
                             Sophia as godhead   (syndrome)

tell me, dear, about the recovery effort (glyphic, strewn)

                         where the first Duma met
              oh things I've been meaning to do:
                    approach attribute what is / to what is not

(Or was that the dula, ouncing toward a birth?)

to what is / again accidental
land of dead letters where
sand ferments box office
treatment down arrow

nevertheless (take five) ultimatums

the children (chain
of associations)
bland me

        spoon   swanee   Tudor-style   moi

The scarcity of detail wherein She (pearls of autumn) transcribes the shadow,
gold in the formula (condoned) by which her night story anti-linear spacing
deepens the *vice versa,* its new tradition (centipedes): your memory's allegorical
march through stone-paved square (notice each perfect edge) entitled to it —
meaning levity—once crawled upon, enticed by A = A forever indifference our
long career of traction and sedatives, our Ivy Hill feast, the parochial "knocked
out of oneself" must learn item order, brakeless steering, forget it nearly as fast
as it startles the other lane into stillness, proximity.

Basis for the risen	static Lazarus
as if	last one up
chamber matrilineal endorsement	perforated is glad ready-set-
tries to cave reply	situated darkened *said*
infatuating	inoculated
long writhe	pupils *danse* they
sanctity dis	purify con
torques me	tractual being
just my latitude	yourself among widths
first person sing	I totaled the worry chord
and you be	you do the same
nary a speck of	least of all a bead
fisticuffs if that	arms a throat
and what you are is	of what you propose
is is the molding on a	could have been crowned

cr	rc
sh	hs
v	v
wh	hw
mantra as	granted fast
Redondo Beach you betcha	ascent at Capri sure as
mayhaps	bedclothes
never liked mythology	pith or preference mirth
too much moisture	fully rain dining on
honest craving for	amethyst and on Hasbro
the toys not toys but	train reenactment
realistic	sadistic
fast or	lap of
slow or	luxurious
here	*brrr*

COMPONENTS OF DISTAL SENSATION (praxis prox-)

leggings, ear warmers, dew-on-demand, smile— say yes

TEMPORARILY DISABLED (refer to the manual for clarity)

I interacted a) never b) a few times c) many times [I replicated answers I had /
you had he(a)rd instinctively an adverb tries to seep in-
to the vale of
gravitational pull (melodious infringement
becomes clarity all (tinglive)
at once)   high frequency
sours the ladder's leap year ring   finally it comes to this   hello, may I help

(you may not; *can you?*) yes, I pro   mise not to come   back   ho   me/pe

lure magma from its trunk   pyroclastic   flagged   under-the-skin
(wince matters; ice shallows in resignation)

She is busy / being pretty / not very much
(herself, you dig?)
sooo urban

Wall off singular regression spates of longing

shrunket viaducts intrude upon our
vice prompts (yellow velvet)
you in muted gold from ribcage dotted Swiss

Is *sinecure* a racist term? I must be without cure. Or applying for double-blind
status and provisions at the gate. She's so, he's so . . . how do you say,
dependent. The same granules of epoxy used to mount a statue can be used to
tip elections, up-surge. The once-plotted day book shorts the month of Feb by
trying to be recent with the purview plunked right where we lose footing
                              wring the smile out of
                                        plaza's predicament remember the twins
Per me si va
                    you know who   lives in that scorched habitat
                                              "the best of times"

              ne la citta dolente

Poverty rests with the outgoing spirit (vastness).

A chess board crowded with fossils
splays
entombment, some
say. The rook envies / wipes out diagonal damage

Your sun is a wing you wear to work
but not even the secretary of grams an amount can
notice because she is frazzled and out of breath
(bringing barges loses large)
or mingles flurry with the sacrament of hesitation

Effeminate, bedazzled predicates let loose our shoulders— A she: (Shri)
                                        fighting to rise
                                        wrestle with all who know

hollow out a ways . . .
        or make assumptions "as you were"
                              skulking around
                              the city of palms
                              inveterate winter   X-game
never stow a frequently used implement

imprinted unequal to imprisonment   inequality   that improvised ritual *de facto*

oversold up to (earballed)

curiously, with glasses

have we any pre-mortem (eyedrums)
medley or memento or emblem to show off?

With only five vowel sounds he managed to induce a coverlet around her
simple shoulders. There's narrative vacancy. Don't point.

Is masculinity a sign of certain hydroxides sugaring the brain?
Is it delicious as forecast? Flatulent.
But . . . is it a perfect fit with license to be radiant?
Is a comma penning you in? Interview the staff, jesus   *hay-zeus*.
                              Ninth street is infertile.
It is noisy to kick at air?
                    Did you hear about her?
How wide is it?

Will it repeat?

How's about a kiss,
he used to say

How about— some pauses even stars cannot convince themselves of. Doctorates
doling out the pink slip eustress. Lock switches key, opposing pantry.

No one visits the file room without telling the guard (the
muscular can't believe its cause   piñata (paint it pink) is
lifted   bard's on duty now [Bay Area Regional Database]
great chain of being   psi-signal digital elevation model
astray   a luminosity

Tank(ed) top(ic) precise N.B. shuffloff
(take three)
natch snicker (recuse)
selves sniffling
on account
of

At the precipice of (spiced) pink:

Forklift (white	you won't do it
Song germ (gray	you will do it
Portico (yellow	you won't do it
Shame (strong	you will do it
Forth (bronze	you won't
Text (url	you will
Lipo (whirl	you won't

By chance *clumsy ants,* are we exciting ourselves (exited) out of delectable permutation? *Ted, paging . . . Is that you? Ted?* As long as I have known you, machine-extruded, the brick falls (you lower it) repeatedly. He bleeds, she bleeds bees from a head wound, merchant mariner, latecomer figurine. *This is my odyssey. This is your perk. I'm drying. Don't get up.* Remnant lucky as the breakup of cantatas . . . It was a wonderful night in Punxsutawney, the gray area I slept on (fleece) saw discord lose its headstart. *I would have flown you to a flower had I known. Sunk my forewing in, midgut and nerve ganglia, everything gained from the original pollen and taut cellophane cavity.*

Eunice was her name
She navied me   *I asked for an axe*
She eagerly   *followed gaping*
She watusied   one must be *gnarled*
She endeavored   one must be *willing*
She was it   one must be *the same* as gnarled and willing   land of the free

I would have helped the concept north. I would have traded out the reeds for silkworms. I would have noticed plurality. Mass takes no time at all. *Those are her words. Where are his words? Where do I fit (glovingly)?*

Few own their damages, my skate key, your skate key. *Watch me.*
Is this rink a dove place? May I watch?

Dim revenues Lolita their way southerly, n'est-ce pas?

Ce chat est bleu
Dustwrapped (plink) violet bands (ampersands) in transit mime our stripped limbs, the arrangement we had fixed. Don't nix the quality methods born from

slack. Melodic underbelly aspires heretofore a pharynx, a creed or limit. (Sing through your nostrils!) In a fit of prescient nominatives, she swore not to attend to magistrates or marginalize their fig addiction, but to paint each strand silver on principle. Whose marine comportment could be a school zone speed limit, an unstudied heart. (Tree bark simplifies this photograph of radishes, its tongue-white rudiment acts as moist proof, sulphate gulf hypothesis red as a crematoria clamorous and rising, staggers back, rising, not letting up or dropping structure). Take three steps, another two, *shhh* moths that drip against stalagmite ration cannot be disturbed. They must drink specific gravity and pH-balanced pear juice, droppings, mausoleum stairs crumbling. (Explain yourself!) Pedagogue entrained but not as fresh a pair of eyes.

Hurry down: we're early soon

Canticles embellish hereby (nearer) frost. Sell bells charm the flocking off the dimwit tree lit frenzy of a holiday light stanching impulse after grotto light. The slight detention theory ruminates about a glimmer while the stowed fresh evidence occurs to mainline stone. The lottery has lozenger properties, so much for loneliness. The maturation point seems solid as a hutch. You butterscotch your way forward and I remain in your due diligence debt economy. She purrs fashionably while you multiply the colic prattle, the quintessential volumes. *Are you there, oh Mildred, our lookout, dearest mortician, page of sleep-deprived dream quadrant densities?*

Raving lunacies lament the mood of Sudan and otherwhere. Storm goes unwarned. One peasant watches like a mother, swung around by the collar, or one butcher learns to be a father, or the one cleaved, who stays a child, who cries out to the nip/tuck shadow: "You! Take a face!"

You cannot reverse downcountry (sublet, succor) (Juliet) this settlement of key tones, splurging just to document the west, make it warmer. Toast the toffee, behave like violins in woodwind-certain heat. Margin calls revamp our suds. I have a bridge to sell signed by Mae West or some other alias. *In loving memory* proudly sponsors the lay-up. Final chance. Don't forget name recognition.

I am truly your young owl. Wise from the get-go, left mid-snow. I trail your spears and sulk back into how it was.

Pure silk is what we dive for
      Duan   huddle up
      Ti   tabby frame

Ge	georgette
Ni	clear, bright, close, loose

Guess what, fey rivers swing back to rubble, are real, have girth, give ground, straighten up to take orders. I turn to starch, yearn for a different sadness, one without timeouts. The stubble on his kissed face told my story to the cadre. I turn the perennial victim to ragweed, poppy flower. My channel says blank screen. A member of our studio audience has just completed his autonomic thesis. When I learn who the committee members swear they are, I'll start to read. Capstone cur- / life raft / scouring pow- Off the record, a sixth division: *Ralph Spartacus, wearing nothing, come on down!* Cameo appearance a meteor logician scribbles on her nap's burned screen a race for three-year-olds. The etch-a-sketch sounds holy as a deaconess. Hellenic fallguy staggered twirl. Whose venerable stasis deserves to be unwound. My unwool raises the specter of your winter silk. The power-at-hand is ineffable. You are registered or associated with a state-run emergency, the Brythonic or Devonian languages removed and stamped: KNOW THYSELF (shake down everything) *hmmm, but* . . . . cherish while you're apt. Immerse me in your gravity. Send signals without cloth. These are all viable expungements. The oath of office means you're only one-third divine. Remember, a relative is reinvigorated in broad-leafed estuary.

Guess whom I ran into? The objective case! Clever girl. I present to you a wooden gland. Make sure to take care of it. Don't let it grow unmotivated.

Saddle-bearing, lobe-finned, do you form your legs on retainer, populate the granitic land? Pre-pangea, winking is an expired behavior, a classic symptom of plus-worthy stems. If you think warble (marvel at the cost), you'll self-medicate outside teach point of anticipated theft. Redeem opponentry from its strapless art staring down a garland of inlets

Densa welcomes you! There's always space for one more like you!

When she's dry, we'll learn the mermaid poses are semi-pretty. Her chance of escape, 28-day recovery, promises— less than 50 percent. Whose metrosexual doors will have lighted every doily shredded on the blockhead and burnt the dialed operation twin unit housing.

Observee name: The premise of being, having been (traded to the Bucks)
Observation period: Tuesday Afternoon at equinox (radiator fluid on low)
Activity: Pompous paradigm trods lightly on Baking needs (but this is

equidistance

balmy conditions working Match point (faultline)

> idolatry gives way to vortex after virtue's
> shot to heck as a long slide into dull wit white hamlets cave outward
> foil the best-laid irritant slowly

> chilled

Once there was a trickle of good faith in the future glutton. S/he spoke less softly than often. And our virtue (as an entity) grew sour. Sometimes people coughed into their elbows independent of one another. Seeing this, I felt immediately free (of what). Be true to virtue. Be less inclined toward your own behavior. After all, the mittens of our body chemistry barely afford our higher grade of trinketry.

Only by a slack inducement did the hurt come to the fore. Retinues entired our frost lane as if contentment forked the road in such as way as to detract from spaces to be chosen. Ritual emblazoned on another person's heart means you are furred and I am frittered, duped, and the landlock of our ocean pricks the feeble out of pretense known as service. My hurt, that is the coupled plaintext slur. Your way of driving home the practice point. My shivers. Your home run. My refusal to move out. Your deck chair when the moon rises. To your long legs. My opiates. Your derivation. My thanks. Your odd craft issuing the committee nod. Your eyestrain. My plump (banned) brimless index. Your stent skimmed off the laurel border at the point of meantime. Nobody is neutral ever caught on the take

fetching Extremities they divide us and concur (ovarian what?)
swell the Malicious fading impulse IQ plinth
Dior fume Fading (oh, he's textured as *manger)*
    expert opinion Proxima projects what telltale pulse (you're listing to the left,
my keepsake)
Maiden voyeur tantamount to privilege offers to spray salt across the pre-ex
    weather.
Tahitian darkroom *l'orange* Imagine being (filled in blank soapbox gala
    butane waterlogged pitcher fruit – a very crystalline approach to damages
left in the legacy
they Recognize (what is already there) standing in your way
a foal in cloth, youngtown slings Enrolls in training as if
groaning Posture among peers

mouths off Pretend adolescence is a custom   subject to review
     clutch play   the hormonal rupee   status quo   this pneumonia lasts
long enough to have been criticized for selfing where a share cost one point
five eight USD (parsed annoyance)

Play coy to the tune of wall CRAWL
street tupper DUCK
wearing on my nervous Riviera
nature (natch) goes bankrupt
affords some bald thing covering
comatose estrangement ceases
to appeal to
witlanes outbound crash through concrete
I'm afraid I admit it You Are The Divider overpass
of the rattler's father role the checkered ash sculptures dotting Pompeii

If (anyway) I were to sock away some plenary fulfillment (just for you) what
would the outcome be if the Maldives were dependent on serving sizes of
paleozoic sand bars, extreme portions, wintry mixes and knock-down grudges
drugged

Superintendency   yes, ma'am supersedes electrifies the ailing happily ever after
doped and strung along flipper its thin fluids hit stride *Lockstep*   *dot dot*
dot   in tatters   splurge the mauled ironworks   less inclined to *Drizzle*
more or sometimes less   *always sunny on the other side of*
                    the same coin   *is it always zero at the tip?*
what *Plate* do you suppose they might serve *tilapia   cherry compote*
stalling   *in circulation*   a "borrowed" patient
Invective   issues from a definite contraption: *is*
a debate erupts over the   first   American thirst *Sorting*
  its bio-degradable prisons   *October fear*   the pred-prey *Vampire story*
          recreates volition
knoll-private tasered *Cheatlist*   what was *Sacrifice*
but a trying time   a *Social intellect*
"becourse" control freak tingles with
having won already

occlusion's not exactly what we came for (did you?)
let's document the intermission   put your cell on vibrate or turn it off

Ready?

    A)   stun gun abnegated
    B)   waterfall or DUI
    C)   chimp dialectics
    D)   lazy beads double-barreled
    E)   mature redhead seen from the inside
    F)   clasped jewel last-stand charge the hill

hating the term "sweet spot"
for the embarrassment
gunpowder (nothing sweet about that)

A crimping of the natural release (cholesterol)   the salt dissolved
      the system full of softened reason (implicate)
  smithereens of quilted slow pace   made to order

caution is a caption
closed for the cups and wands
the anti-trust hearing: show business

We're very plural anyway (not fractal) and drawn out with rain, pier lancing
fog (heated on runways). How many millennia? *Call for the question.* The great
day is . . . upon us. Mechanical failure, a trick of water, chad nets and whaling
routes, not as prophetic as say when we needed the resource, were burned at
the hearth for it. *Elemental, period. What to do about morning*

                Relief.

Blasé repeat zones in a quandary (plick
Poultice preyed upon, sticks and sand will break (stricken
Open the body's best   cryptogram (flickering
Defense (unbroken
Skin) against the accepted breathing protocol
                    Unchallengeable
        failsafe

Our curse: scarlet tea oils, our television crystals lying flat on snowy napes.
Spray is cured, goaded inward, splashed before we can technologize the velcro
troughs this sea rakes over its approval process at every continent *entré*

Shaped me with salt and gave me six more months   to live
Within the bath   so that everything water can do eyes do
The scuffs came undone (will be unveiled) rebuff the tongue   it has
secondary significance   The leavings meant   blinking   central
division   WARNING this relationship is not going well   Me, only
I slip like you do
except that I separate   Partially undone   evolve rigidly   from capital
rivers   rafters lowercase Opiate distortion   fruited   episodic
Vamonos   *Eleanor*   (that is not an option you have)

My surface is your ivory mansion
cucumber extract sprayed across blistered skin
              the sun loves us   poisons us   does not apologize
for its UV crimes

She said *talk to me as if I were someone else*
you spoke to nicely

I live for what few dorsal fins I notice when I weigh the earth

                                    (bag it)

And then the purse strings soft as craned necks contract around broader
strokes. *I'd like to see . . .* Surely you watched the palladium rid itself. Throw
open its human side to derision, even paradise. Curses reclaim symptoms of
maternity, plans a media fair how they

march in brittle fours   hop
                  stochastic   to-it
recency

                        Entangles   Stirs the pot so-to-speak   at Valparaiso
If I wear a helmet why don't you embroider dreadlocks I imagine I will grow
unless the bald look is *appropriate*   *or* subject is discovered
                                        did you hear?
              The object is the game
              of obsolete objects   *I object*
              itself the I: or S: drive   matters little in this culture of
                              prediscovered *fin de*
                              subservient
         danger level of warm ill-defined place —internal—

In a rinsed way the arbor day afforded a matriculation
Similarly bay's dialogue fodder for a decade into it
Similarly roving wind, raving don't you mean?
Similarly articles endowed with dissimilar
Curt wigs renege
Majored in (airpo) hypothesy (rt)   think "human resource"

My metronome is in the closet.
Your metrognome is in our hut.
What is the distance between ¾ time and any daddy's hurryup?
        Picking you up from school was the best decision he might have never
made.

His hesitext would soon import a strain of violets (crisscrossed), engulfing the
akoya, the fresh hutch grasses (letter perfect) just up, stretching and stooping.
To learn, the market blends aluminum with insult. Eyelag exhibits marginal
self-control. Her diamond said the sports guy means her intellect is shored up
once the crinoline is left to melt apart from bucketry. The instant message TTYF
stings pearl coaxes early bloom *read the last row* provision's reticence. UV
undermined to offer (undermind) the leafage broadband silt. Swift current
repairs awareness (suffrage), but not before farms culture jasper from façade.
Alarms melt manufacturing plots within earshot. Stilts buckle whenever help is
on the array. The artificial decal, a person or anemone, an outcropping of rocks
jabs the strophe *you there, yes you*. Go there shielded, find a village— *I want to be*

Impinging on (that is to say) the larimar ping
your freckles (recently) relent sanctity
Approach but beware (compare frigidity) of the dog

and other flings   thou shalt not park here   a truism
            I've heard it has several states of mind
Bewildering demarcation (fatuous) on
steel pan (*noticias*) desultory Provencal
underpinning limber (past tense) lassitude
as care prays for remitting
serpentine O protected
      gentle imperatives
        go   stay
the ripe blue summer pattern hinges on
verges though frankly I would bide
my time if storied pitch

let me go on good faith [feyth]
                    1. confidence or trust in a person or thing
                    2. belief that is not based on proof

Continue to repave all summer moon glow in apprenticed heat
She serves well these allusions impending
And when I hear them there are adages to feign
                    is your birth certificate a telegram
                        lady-in-the-box
                            which half?
Although there seems no difference between shelf life and jail time
The troubling winter
Nested near the part of me young as
Silver coated breaking news

*When I nest, will you agree not to have faltered? I need your breath. I point to rest
until the often ivory coating breathes back into our homework. Once upon a textual
rendition, I became a theory. And you rounded all my corners with your inkblots. One
of them, a bald saguaro, offered little inroads for the furry flowerlings just right for a
hummingbird.*

The lemonade tastes dark again
        spill   shaded sand   noseeums interlace the grape trees
                undulant beau fatale

made those leaves with apple juice concentrate
once   simmered differently
so native make turned   I'm not going
        to ask you again   (sideshow barker) I am a glutton for possessions
distract me please to di(e) late d is t a nc e s
desert all weather let us say   get in or out
and neighbors came to find   unreachable by convention
community on that unsafe   Eva   a- not e-
street where we were robbed   the rough sketch
and they took everything   described meaningfully
except the flute worth more   than what?
than the entire household   <u>no great escape</u>
full of quick sale chintz

None of the closets empty out for you. None of the weeds assure us back that
we are capable of rung tips needing height. If I were anything

109

(like you)
I would have mooded my way south
where all the eagles
sprawl through skylight
and its sparring darkness

Many of the daughters learned to paint their way out
Sheer self and customary charges
Protagonistic airstrip
Shelf life charcoal by letter   tear up $
After all, the pearls were wet, out of tune
The lines were drawn, erased, re-drawn
The candidates available seemed deflated
Topical but mordant
It dawns on you: soon decide
                    the side you'll
                    ride on with me
                    shotgun

Shut UP, one passerby said repeatedly *I've nothing to sell you*

Pain's daunting paint and silver-edged flyleaf wreath hung a bouquet of blood
cylindrical
            grasp for me (host point)   pass over my brief cuticle phases

            dominion (solace)

bland rigor tigers its way sullenly through psyches

and the man who has the poultice in his backpack
won't come near the ICU patient   International Contemporary U-turn
(who *are* you, said the preacher) reformed, of course
resurfacing mirroring his makeshift suspender
patch of face again   afloat
strained insensate pollen (taste center)   concupiscent moons   *why don 't*
you pack it in   vocalize
        cuss at these arboreal foyers   doorbell-crazed
                                    booths a grim restaurant sufism
razzmatazz   *there are certain inhospitable "sections"*   dietary checklist
                                    sí?
My only objective amounts to an objection which in turn amounts to this

qualitative free-zone parlaying of
ribs and notices as fine as
children

Woodwinds
(are not acquainted)
With the depth of brash
Infection
(invective)
Unless protraction
Deafens
One of us

Train ride (visioned) depth percept
Curses the link (prinkled)
Stone high as crept
Up on   one-two-three   *jump if you are*

inflamed (charred) with   Eden   fertilizing cricket song   exothermic
poorly evolved   (hermit on a chair)
fur be   is   or will it   damn this   infusion   this arduous conjugal visit
          or might it be
                              difficult to choose   (mid-air) rough-and-tumble
longing   here   there   what brothers do
elsewise   (and everywhere)   clean our deathbeds with Brillo and lye

Summa cum vortices   *I am the day— I, I, I   full to the upper lip*
                              as with a terrible noise

Stipend rejects person (numbering in the thou-
Wingspan cleanses the third world spigot (rushing forth my down time
Chasten surf contests (cleansed
Score then write a tell-all (prance
Palaz fledge
In flotilla In formation In Alt Control

Sutures comma whetstone
Quotation marks
                              scrubbed launch

brim time limber scorches   badlands, yes?

rapture put off is (breastfed) when it's swollen lonely or lovely I believe I feel
for you

                              and can exist (do we?)
accountably you are not forethought
                              but if you must know
                              yes, I can tie Phaedra (known to her
                              friends as Phyllis) a noose a knot
                              apply a voltage
                              so when she unintentionally
                              rips herself away (disrobes or drags
                                        Act III into that bloviated
                                            ambrosia of plastinated talk
                                                easy as coincidence
                                                    inhabited and brought back
                                                        to sight)

If only folded notes occur (wet into brine)
                    in Chiapas   Rio
On staves I will have
                    parachuted   dined early
Paved the starch with
                    25 million years ago
Recent carping
            "the first of its kind"

I play ocarina preciously
log hours in the manual
the only overdose I ever saw   a pitfall of aspirin
and joint lubricants   no tears   "atta girl"
                    overcame   the braced joy   downplayed our chances

chanting   scrunching (stalagmites   revered
stings   peak (geometric fancy stows our gorgeous hits
opacity   I can see clearly now (strewn seedlings
few wings   more mid-air (say-so infracts
would course   collisions
for timbre's   renewal
outflow   *prove it*

streaks of bevy of interminable yeast infectives
yow sarong
against the cult grill   the audiences of hunger

I'm up against it
I'm pretty happy though
I'm faring for myself
Are you prepared

vinegar provides *what?*
      Baltic permanence
                a city hooked on oxygen

dribs and drabs of chakras mint the nubile rest point
up for grabs

Sad to say the salt priest major flyboy clunking around majestic stints left open
Whole notes lodged inverted intraday
average the perimeter
Of stoking   vestigial
Branch ruins on the brocade of seasoned
Alpine limping
Over there
               Let's think this over
the Yaddo function chalked up   smitten
finished among
                  barrels and hedgehogs
     pincushions and chollas
        prickly pears and the brazen *Lophocereus*
she wove into the lot
and strung a cowbell across the miltonias and firelight jars
numbered icicles   the private drive DO NOT ENTER *les fleurs*

where am I going to find . . .

dots infringe upon laced
feet   are looser than   blood loss

bless me father
with listless lever
              What do I care if you eat fever

At the grotto I hemped
Pay dirt into
Burlap cartilage

Now what?

                                       in a strutsy lawn bowl kind of an
                                       ever-sift
                                       I bought a *you rang?*
                                       chin, nose, cheeks
                                       the plums (Yorkshire) they were
                                       tubular   how we deny each other

What do I care . . . .   strands the should
                                       er strap bookbag marvel
                                       a breed he jethroed his way
                                       to the key notice
                                       this papyrus attrition
                                       bored out of our curriculum
                                       conquistadorish funnybone
                                       distributed function laughed-at
                                       Immaculata came to be the hall
                                       I bounced from bait-and-shadow
                                       communion four hours overdue
                                       a way for   all the way
                                       us to be   moribund
                                       as Corinth   a cop-out

v i v a l a f e v e r s i l e n c e w o r e w o r d s b a c k h a n d e d t h e n w h a t s o
f t n o t t h e r e s u f f e r s m e g l a d l y c r o s s e s a t y o u r o w n r i s k r e n e
g e s o n c e w a x i n p l a y f o r c h e r u b i c t h i e v e r y

Marauders fling their Cheshire shirts for smile's outpost of *huh*
smile's fortissimo   smile (period)   repetitively ask what circle am I in   go on
          goad us
Wampum breeders   sounding more paranoid here's the wrist exercise
push-ups Hosing off the clumsy   allpro developmental mojo   riverfront
overflow between a rock Quirk of fat(e) let's weigh half our options   only half
if we have one, we have twenty
isn't that a phrase you'd prefer And by the way you owe me furniture
                                  ash gets into the vents
                                  people panic   scatter

foolish primacy
rec-
        are we on?
Unless I was asleep when you roused the fire escape which did not come
toward me

114

"a minor flight delay"   stress *minor*

a rugged (trampled) manifest(o)   what it means to be saved from
referrals romance   such a loaded cloud   while there's still news   Removed
dust from the patio   the poster   we must whip and downgrade   cart off the
waiting arrivals   Leaving complicit attitude in place   On placards near the
rose-berth   the clearest minuet   Text

When I see you and I like you then will we be
Thumbing rides to the
Inestimable fortunes of eternity
Or living in a crusty hut
To which we and only we (not us)
Will have twin keys

patched (quick) hind
myth ologic Allah   happy in wartime   all they that take   shall be
                              -iness

Starch starves   affords   a say in
  So what (at this junc
ture

fluid in prefecture
vestments temple pro
forma voluble (chase vehicle)
rich immoral (carnivore) *don't*
herbal fatigue—*do*—sets in that
its threshold for highstep
pillaresque (vitiated) attainments

w   hen
y   ou
p   ray
w   homonym
d   o
y   ou
p   ray2

                    BAR IS OPEN (pass the blank over space what about blank
                              space and how did you space yourself
                              was space blank to begin with?
                              or more space . . . JUST ASK)

Pander to the wheels
life a temp   borrowed
from life we drain
so it goes on

investiture enlists spam
I pile on hurry points   world on notice
The dust restricts my sledge
My landfill and Each latch
And I go mumbling *cameras change the apprehended*
Through the torpor, what about the forests?
To retreat into *yeah, what about them?*
My tone poem   this is not going to work
In a vast anointed   you must be proud
Matrix of deployment   whose son are you
                    am I   hello siren   hello equal oppor-
          family X family Z   redo it all   don't argue   sir moon

At precisely three forty-five that morning, a trailer skidded into
the court building one hundred and forty years between 1932 and 1935
flames shot high self-guided tours
and records were demo
lished discharged
our life was there
within the fake marble
sentencing municipal interdependence
and now without copper price stability
cooling our stove coils the trading floor (red to black and back again)
and from there we race
and we scrape by
Remove the dowels   I hope this evening goes smoothly
Intrude upon the gender bill   repro   duce   But will it hold?
ID after   apprehended   the restructuring   color there is no object
A fashionable promise
Pert and rinsy shirt dovetail fleeting— returns to the same place once twice
three times a Line where the(y) dove under and discovered a woman's privacy
Coat used to
breathe   end in expulsion

court is there for us, although
we have long

since rekindled what
it constituted   *there is a message*

       A mixology   A de *can't* tor (torrent) of
                           tour (our) an orch(estra) id
                                 any graven image (orchidly)
                                 12-slice the anony
                                   (muss) must you be so . . .

Listen, you!
          I will not be spoken to

                              fascist stand-in   extra straw

for her head

Stentorian tonography made matte finito
In a stern way the ranch dressed my
Integrity and now this is my horse you say   no saddle or "breaking in"

Ramblin' man(ner aye Everett) rest

              What Greek letters have you Θ Ω

Rationography nostalgia with spritz of chai
tea tariff plops prowls its way in
To my damaged feed bin   the kitchen wallah

barren   cinema no longer (white sill) will accept invalidated stubs   (tub
of sop) no refunds will be given under (are we prone) no shirt no shoes
sorry   any circumstance *do you mean any?* the forest is endemic (has come
down with something) thanks for the memories   the washout

se me olvido
new winter
already priced
out of my range

     The hare's eyes nesting penetrate you (quasi) or are dust storms.
Newfound balance. This is my greening wound (asparagus the steam risen
        the pot dark)

A confederacy of (anything writhes). What an exceptional wilderness
this turned out to be. Stingalong might endorse force nick of time
romantic option.

Spring jumpsuit of bulbs burning nine nights.
The lap-size float. The Turkana boy (his voice).
What is this crackling you claim to know flow said to damage
pathogenesis

its midnight mint   ziplocked for freshness born-on-
dating is the superfluous muttering of sideline waterfall
along the great gorge   engorgement
Yay is written but not banked
vegetation will conserve its diesel
table proves beyond reasonable
delight

I laugh chuckle at the off-color suffix
When I redress
My moments
And then earn them
Back pogrom disintegrates IQ

Waft goes ultimo
Sugar defies (defines?) Ottawa
The lamplight   I love you-nots along Thames
tabular little gems fog considers you empty   third-degree
(redaction fraught with)
Curbside *check this out*
Now is the tiempo
Temporal and stowed for future enhancement
Purple   pious   mother lode

he lost his son in the process
emotive eyes
sacrosanct luster
far down

we're off   we're off   we're off   reset your vertical if you can   follow the
follower

Embellish *whinge,* that is to say, portent of pretense crossed away. Fire's first
injurious moor slung over shoulder(-length) attunement yet entwined in razor

shrapnel confiscated slurry of mistakes. If I were yang and you were yin, if I were partial to a thin eclipsing of the large, what would you tell me back to shutter slugged resistance to the petty rain? In a moment, there are protests, protrusions

She lost her runaround new flight of stairs

sleet is undergrowth

And the courtroom blasphemy will have sealed off its avocation
And the doormat crimson otherwise will have refused its WELCOME
And the stiff noon parch abandoned its executive summary, contesting your
       draft inductee
And the pilot light of lung trouble faltering blown out will have *wished* the
       emissary good luck
And the insecticide of greed added later for stock and flavor
And the rework grafter spilled like Samsonite over first-, second-, and third-
       place field day ribbons   medals (mettle?)   as in "she had a field day"
       with the coordinated attachés
              (synonymous with attacks)
And the hobble kissing I met you faked for laughter   thread and needle
       whiskey   horticulture outlawed   their bulky hybrids   equal time
       for diplomacy and disappointments
And the hobby prone to and of languages   broken ranks   treasury chest
       cards   hydroponics the study of air mail   runway furor   let
       out   *let us go*
And the elbow room abrasive shortened   *projectile*   shoulder-to-shoulder
And the attraction of ameliorative shut-down   the last ditch effort
And the knowledge versus faith curtailed   freshened fast
And the tone of my indenture deflated   querulous   no more than a
       means to an end
       of future means   reassigned if and when inappropriately
       touched / mishandled   darling relic   the century older   "passing by"
       pièce de résistance   junk

There is inconceivable loss
whoever's in charge must record

paper factories and classmate searches
MORE TO interact
THE POINT with

ADVOCACY the hype
GROUPS think
tortoise-like gymnastic
hip-to-hip
maneuvers rot

ROUTINE INSISTS US INTO SQUARING OFF
ONE OF THESE TIMETABLES I AM
GOING TO RETRIEVE YOUR DUST
THE FUSILAGE IS TOO LONG TO BE VIABLE
PAID FOR AFTER
ALL YOU HAVE CON
TRIBUTED

a promo tional   tension (fist like) we desist from perfume to parfumerie.
I must respectfully decline / take you up on your exaggeration. Somebody do
*some*thing intelligible, an able simplex, jumping from entertainment to world to
weather to news to business to the crestfallen (when) call center. Informing
your consent to   test result   frightened   network   bartered for stable
access, if you find this product unsatisfactory, stale. I already predicted the
restart later centigrade milieu, retreating when the plows died. You forgot
to return your half for keeps (my minnows in the laundry recently dissuaded
from their nevermind rotation), drawbridge openings bludgeoning the frozen
rental contract (clause ???), my imported ointments wreaking (samples
intubated, expiration date xx/xx/xxxx, revelers flocking to the shattered quiet)

She married *him*? (recode the evidence; incinerate yesterday; revelate)
What happened to the red tulips on the windowsill?
The vintage annual report   gone away
The park is closed   a slur
And many waxen images   bereaved we assert
indent Young (youth) guesses   with passing with a
pointer

Nurses like short-sheeted powders— *nice to meet you*   pass flat-eyed
grumbling about days off and the room at the end of memory   glass under
bare   floor neatly folded   heels at the end of
                                        the imperceptible district   cotton
                                        seed suppressing itself   swarms
quip and spasm   calf twitch   *this is not real nor is it skin*

              our deaf supervisor
              shiftless (shirtless)
              technician of unproven claims   Oh but the
effectiveness of it

Can you identify the caller? "Do not call" haunts impractical living. You take
this, that, the other. You go bland and trade space for space, spouse for spine.
You, You, You
2-for-1 nights under the feng shui parallel. Posit graves. Depose the false chart,
graph, morphology (it *could*) progress, however, not likely. Stir martinis to our
sun's detriment, the plain opener for business and letter perfect transportation,
mid-April. Not comical in the least.

I propose an a propos filmed toast to the passengers
we cannot get away from living fabulously in
whatever it is   inquires   brags   believes
the tender offer (croppes) never (not in my lifetime or yours)
will expire. Thus far, the woodwinds have avoided
the edge, the undercooked huevos, and the upper intertwined
guard. Nobold(l)y cares about the double reeds, snapped, burnished, shrinking
the neighborhood, the drum cage, the clean-up crew, the outcome

Nobody gambols or gambles for that truffled
              extension the HUMAN *arctic brazil* spreads ISM
              sodium enrichment over metallurgic slot wheel fabric
              snuffing out elegant odors
              cleverkey dungaree kneepad made-to-order holes
              waterproof wind-resistant beneath public scrutiny embellish
this

(matter inflames gold silver bronze substitution of labor min/max/ideal
              elimination round the national who-cares
              ensnared in ABC stride residuals
              athletic but unnatural

Tattletales will have been bred
In time for their efficiency to take
H O L D the Jacuzzi like "so"
snubnose is the name they award you if you miss

                    DON'T MISS

the vital nutrient
intensive care
tides revert

Him (salty): *Oh you're here. I didn't think you'd show up.*
Her (monopolized): Where else would I lay myself down? Is there another
                    Alexandria you've heard of? Didn't think so.

      Caller's name and social, birth and death, family history, stance on
      purgatory
      does it exist does it not   does she love me anyway? slashing costs on
magnesium printouts— oh it's a good book, the glow, the firm, the famished
    medley, you should read the page numbers out loud, but don't make
        eye shadow threats pure as
      climactic Late Show danger Okay let's be completely
        honest with one another

repeating one
Spanish-influenced
language word the two have no
formal bloodline at a time under
~~duress~~
make that *direction*
shafts travail *(en ingles)*

Juridical huckster a poor sport   (pour *alert me* docked) plod, plod, plod along
synchrony is Minutiae and you cannot get around the escrow
spiritual predominance on account of you, more for her
                         less for instant gratification (him)
     a childhood rearing his upbringing offers sandbags numbers
     (loses everything   amplified)
Of flavor and house fire   a boat with eighteen children capsizes Somewhere
pugnacious smoke
the "safe" design

Satchmo, right?   you've recognized me!   *maybe*
        kind gentle never kind never gentle
      during ignition the sequence starts over
        a manner of postponement
                  God

Impedance   let's be discrete   and oh dear   so wrathful
Paint for Bruce
raise the smog alert
            lead level
            euthanasic

a cannery at Limoges
And tattoos don't
palliate what they intend
                                pain— can reinforce

Remake heaven in my image so I'm certain
To get in   self storage   the cold machine a room is
      distant breakfast of cantaloupe and fennel   antiquarian   bland bisque

The lake is full of princess charm and the narcissist
      is impassable   waiting for your praise   what's meant by a good secession
            way to go   pat on the wing
      you'll be something   someone   else
bereaves collective going-down
where it is likeliest to venture
peace-proof and apart from
the mature intention
various and skimmed
alongside cerebellum legroom an amenity or braless

I haven't conjured you in weeks
I fear you wear the robes of the child's inimical gazelles
  worshipped into sacrifice   stalking her   if she had one
  medicinal purpose   would cheat at this creation

            where is the release, the hatch

(marginal regalia falls under the wheel-bearing recycled wads of clay
time owns time, clay pitched into the middle of tundra
moving under its own cloud   for protection   for growth potential

no one will bother it there   Eve, Eve, Eve

(if I fall into heaven it will be a proxy scat sing corner office with floods of
  elective sing-along which can make a sad person even sicker of themselves

acorn, come out of your shell   bird of a color: soot   two in the Hyacinthus
Orientalis anchoring alternative rosebed   contrive yourself

ghazals grip not once but twice
find me a bazaar or a goatee that isn't being worn by a Shylock
I can have it trademarked   on demand

(very many advocates drop their cause in the end stages; they forget the
protocol

(tonsure: gleeful clerics   coastal memorial   after its peak

(fat cha agh pah   sounds?

(lolly folly you are my *ochema,* you are my *ka,* you enter posh hotel bars at
whose
        request

(gratuities you think a society wrests from you your dubium

(for keeps, you are my *paradeigma* film squints over the Balkans

(relinquish defining image

(mollify the warrant   now add savings   supreme desire

                                                    Vest in just this isthmus
(dappled where the perks are   *I can't keep my eyes open*

(radar from the deceased   bats   there is a darkness in them   toy bones
compiled see a compilation at cave's bottom   projected onto yellowed and
unreadable privacy filter   the miner's flaring helmet

            esse is *percipi*   the other way?

(findings. I send you null hypotheses like tiny fretboard husks: thou shalt not

(shut up and play

cha
quicken

basting   ----- whatever I choose it to mean, neither more nor less
chaff   (ex-head)   the One and Only

Hers isn't heaven | | table the equivalency | | table when
I'm mad I still | | expunge the river | | walk with me
To tirade | | all throughout Milwaukee | | I was born in Red Bank | | town at
the foot of Hecatonchires (cheers), consigliere, director of photography | | I rest
my small head in Borogroves | | I will picture till my depth | | lands a hundred
hands and fifty heads away | | Your face | | the angel of imperatives | | reigns
over my possibilities | | sidetracked almost as if | | I had bedraggled my way
through linguistic | | rabbit hole compost | | Chump change and retreated
for good | | to a city where | | not a syllable | | survived | | Familiarized
my fate | | and every statue was from Norway | | chill rides up | | Every piece
of continent removed me from it | | altogether practical | | six foot poles | |
new jabs made me | | confident | | because the weight | | because the weight
room | | Cadre of imposters | | made me wait for | | wait on | | hostess Sakyo

Over to the heft point was a man named Tom, plain, hard-working
No worse off than
what I'd read / volumes on the mountain
                    pages that could have
                    filled a jeweler's eye
Playing strewn scrap metal cast-offs voted out, a despot
                    dumping ground
Spoons rehashing their handles
                    foibles bottom feeding
To midriff our collective
Way through musical
Diversion
                    osis- flop of A

Notice brackets tends to precede interrogation
Points. Central Intellect

Notice nothing else.

                    Water moccasins
                    Blackheads
                    Hognose
                    Bull

fetch the boy   violins wrestle
give him an apple stem and oar
      and ask him why they derive from similar materials
so abject the northern night might hunger for vegetable   mineral   or star
   human choice   indemnified against it   fear is a consideration, true   WW I
II-III-IV-V (occlusal)   Udjat: vaulted eye (victorious!) heals   without Sekhem
or his honor's say-so

> sun-disks erupt in
> mega construction
> foreman fodder
> between 36th and 37th Streets
> Nekhbet, be my protectress
>   come with me to the gymnasium dance

At night the flower dangling from your wrist closes and hums. Ba, your flail
      and crook are showing. I'm not ashamed. Should I be?
The rubies I was given were not bookish things.
The gem show's past. I wonder if the firelight will get all over me.
The breath you will reassure others with, the primordial hill, the dung beetle's
      spontaneous creation.
The lion's share, head cloth, the loin crown my heart
The seat time   has departed
The injurious rosy abrasion cetaphil will assert   rate the rater   raise
Incompatible with(in) reach   the potter's wheel   arrow pointing to lung
inhales snow lathering the ficus   webbed palm, your dandruff-studded snow
replete with knots and blood   feathered tiaras and fetish   breach-filling
scepters   cracked jar of pigments   our shelter   sistrum   sister horseshoe
jackal to the herdsman   falcon tears   they mean to give life *canis majoris* your
scrappy shrine   ascends every seven hours for a beautiful rest   speechworthy
if you insist (tired yet?)
      Which number renumbs you?
      You rue the chin, protagonist of Munich
      the turvy way. Sure, wire your pruned hand . . . we'll see

Your seating will take place at two minutes past ten o'clock. Dimensions of
your conversation have been pre-recorded. Three coronets, the fourth a
violation (be ready) announced by the top authority. Frivolous moving
violations, last ticket to St. John (around midnight)— oh don't they go *on* and
on. Assistance, the handicap, the smirk.
I don't usually float. Dixie cups of Demerara rum distributed broadly at the

lodge. There's a strong, silent count. Moral gray handfuls, less an advantage to be had. He's feeling quite relieved, beat-around-

[Commisery: be real to me, bent from laughing]

If I can . . . street ball, what a safety pin and stick could do in the grimmest instance. I don't think it would be *right* to threaten. I'm not claiming to be the diva, the fortune teller leaning in so the mice won't hear. (They do, regardless). I get my motivation by delaying talks on such a sensitive subject. I am trapped.

Geeky shoulders nab the 20/60 eyesight (whisper to
Authority to see (will it be limited follow me wherever I cough, stagger
The frost amounts to a plush asymmetry needling the confit (comfort) as we
Steam our wits and breathe our most (in)accessible dateline
Next thing you know the neighbors have enlisted us in suds egg-harvesting
studies

Textual restraint afforded by
The whimsy of a drift through which
I crawl to meet the regulation
Diagram trinket intellect for tribe on tribe
To rib us "has spoken" *leave now*
Offering Sparta the Ninth Ward the Emblazoned
What next

3.

This ice flower showing in the lens
has not been touched yet by wind.
One looks toward edges of the flower
at the fragile petals framing what precedes
a formal tension sensed looking at time
not as a bookmark clothing rigor in the pose
defining species and the moment and the stage in life
through which one knows the thing seen
presuming that its hue includes the crease.

You excoriate the jubilee and invoke flowering as a basic term. You ought to be
familiar with yourself. Featherweight aspires to but not for: *size may appear* ready
as an attaché left unattended and is resorbed. She goes there again. In rigorous
places you stumble deeply into foxglove. Stageground is block print. Dress-down
the charade.

forgiveness wintering toward
blue small idiolect
imposing afterlife

The amaryllis molts uncontrollably flaps
in the looseness of its edges its fractured frame
substantiates engages the petal and
closes its airway for a lasting pose. We mark
the affidavit read tack it to a pillory. *We hope*
what's ordinary has come to this. The fruit of
ice jags under our tongues. Eyes reject
when dawn ignores itself who can complain.
The azalea flames out mixing companion with company.

Feckless safe-appearing dunces hopped up on fermented grapes assume their
turn at bat while playing clean. Their being in the lead routinely pillories validity.
What is the eye for if not to gather poses interposed with what may last? To nix
the armrest loses an inborn substantial hedge. Meanwhile tongues refrain from
proclamation.

dining room chair
ensnares Creole ether
premeditates son daughter

Lotion tames us in keeping with

the stall a lone one whose optic nerve
adjures a recollection. Timing paints us shut
and rungs are climbed to locate injury where
eyesight will not have vied with sleep cost.
Growth repeats to wind the mind gathered
by affidavit springing to attention via
cardinal virtue of choice in tune with
an emerging dawn substantial in grade and weight.

I is thine rule of all rules. Pay little heed to wash 'n go editing its percentage and
spoken rate best effort fell behind where behind feels uncredited with last ditch
aspect— *tariki* this other person sharing my bed pointed sanitized. I want a word
here instead of letting myself waterfall ingrain as an arrow wakes to its referent. -
ix for the noise of you.

> sanity not sanitized
> word implies reason
> granular if fact

Like emergent properties slower motions
flip the crew cut. I could have predicted you
seat filler set extra your flow shut off
protensive contact with those who brought
vices stiffening the order. Gold ladders
deceive by blast. A growing boy and girl
prying each other open with one-liners safer
stimuli for vorticism hand-washing
rituals rollaway beds and paper bows.

Placid is not motif thus. The diphthong of canary plush as scent and *ought* to fend
away *jiriki* not at all the gold elastic motile eye. Whose lungs open while we roll
toward the merging of distended a cappella frocks I'm trying to place the raft in a
safe stream for him to know there is life in air brushed forward by the lines held
true to ritual.

drive-by porcine lies
the abated years
where we capitate

Encyclicide remands antagonists as cut
crews hold off overwork. Grade A-tions

lift the order to a wash troy ounces flatter
the collective and a single stimulus for patching
'ainthood might prescribe a toast to pry
out folkways lingering where songs
have ledged into troika pillowing
a sage rush texting lifeblood to ER
presume someone knows the steps.

Trodden signs fuse blending comfort with thematic brunt. Bold banshee bamboo
somatoform I stab at the bar-space arsenal slick with enfamil whose foreclosure
posts and comments on tempura aftertaste or in other words vocal chord attrition
robbing the convenience from granger. Swept down to split stump deforested
laugh track attic.

> lowering elation from
> coded bars sweating
> the evasive stuff

Spots cycle past astringent tasks fill orders.
I fumble for change the A +/- symmetric love
letters thought: I ought to put off illustrations
in favor of expenditures filmstrip matching
miniscule contributions. The cutting room floor
calls what father says and mother parrots
out of touch so why am I always looking
down a hallway comparing our inside voices?
Drawl rears up in place of your choosing.

Sleigh feel to the downspout and a latch to hold the film on. This amounts to
trawling rosters of expenses as if and only if fumbling for cuttings can be done
without a floor. The change one seeks is hybrid and comparatively is not a voice.
In smallest increments they shirk their looks. A favor is equivalent to string left
theoretical unless amended.

> stood up for
> par four they
> inch apart afraid

Episodes give not a blink of raw relief.
Recall being sentenced to a book.
It was belief that capsized match-making

through the summer gloss finish on the cusp
of faltering from pictographs in dapper
father to a father to a father
within earshot of the sidelines where
adventure ribs the young apprentice
who makes his living looking striped.

Nicks the crown for if one loses a foot to shredder notches another crawlspace
among cedar noises. Fosters cheer subject to inspection and sparing them the
trouble. Cantankerous this elementary dash— going to improve lowercase art
group circles surround worksite precaution exits coursing over bountiful lots.

finishing adventure in
a lather inter
alia quipped thing

Epistemology if conditions of surrender
sew strikable air pockets. A gamut raises
acetone-taut captions "the hackles" addressed
pater noster. Reflex invites his guilt into you
where sinking is a snow advisory a made-up
encounter bronzed reflected with one brush
of ceramic elbow. Haste buries today show
phonics. Refreshed warehouse fails us
beautifully. Handle *laude* with caution.

Adverbs laud advisories sans *hush*. Wheat fields no longer show. Trills of breath
evict the substance of apparent knowing in favor of a brush with song. If
pocketed intelligence is deemed a gift it's still ceramic against harsh ceremonial
indifference. Sound allows for striking distance in or around the midline rushed
for purposes once counted slowly.

flauta of coinage
wasted tulip god
crooked or unfair

Rushing to advise makes up for sinking feelings.
Ontology lifts pocketed bronze while honoring
the laudatory housing amid snow. A fresh coat
maintains stills. *Qui es in coelis* speaks
only to reflecting years of daylight

over the hidden and visible nouns alike
surrendering to sonorities spoken or restrained.
Care is taken when mistaken footfalls shift
the air the wares script above it all.

If we had fingers instead of lips and verbiage instead of protest. Evince "it's all
been done" line by line drag strip entre vouz a statistics of betrayal on six-month
leave. Destructive tenacious impertinent yes no maybe. They appear nonplussed
even though we share the same water source. Meaning lightens the burden
where loathing shrinks.

daylight lit by
mention beloved mistakes
goodness of fit

Who approaches is it Leith your shaky attempt
at rescue? Consider yourself one of us rubbed
invisible quickshot— a year in the life. Take
the ingénue on her word renew her adjectivity
(oceans you grow *or grew* careful in). I often wonder
about sound's possessive whether it will reveal
the ringleader herd the excesses the triplet routine.
Waterborn one accepts the possibility that heavy
metals do not behave well under rectilinear pressure.

Perpetual possessives fail to yield to scepter. Watch induction of the posse and
call upon routine to pare durable goods from terra firma. Is there rescue in the
cards? Platonic overtones writhe with melody's substantial influence. The leader
lacked capacity to chortle thus reflected upon rings of hell. No tears welled in or
near dim sense of either sight.

insolvent crate spawns
disorganized affair our
tope excuses form

Press the water to refine the flock. Cattle triple
routine chores. Taking the lead these spare parts
whatever's left of what will be remembered.
One projects the sound of the award the person
nanoquick new photographs looking rarely round.
To behave is to be lacking in imagination or

to convince the modified to accumulate more
prop words might mean rings around the cozy
for the nonce and *better dresses* with a flounce.

Ice flower in sap amplifies take-out wedding march the crushed sun index finger
hunt-and-peck repairs polarity. Coined dynamic. Part of parts strains and there is
an incredible outblowing follows definition and search word love (in practice) so
what one doesn't want one does. A guest applies matrimony to fire the sides of a
storm.

> ecce sound flocking
> modified cozy polarity
> about face guest

With each successive wail the cradle scallops boredom.
I don't particularly care if I juggle synonyms blinding
my fuller self but of course falling is a private matter.
It takes patience acting cold. Or if rock bottom deepens
the operating theater let us not immediately trade alibis
ask a forest to obfuscate boiled ginger with quotients
of meridian cured laid in rows numbered. Count to three then
search revamp swap partners restore vociferous dreams against
the laparoscope and mold its bow-legged subjects into lowercase.

Only the act of following makes clear what failure means. There is no alibi for
certitude. It shows the way a scope returns a verdict more precise than dream.
At the bottom of the ninth a cold wind cures meaningless amperage disguised as
courage or an original line of code. Behold the trees subjected to these reams of
force field under analysis.

> redwood winter my
> paradigm of gold
> writing this off

Private begging needs to rest in neat and nearby rows.
Rock bottom rocks becomes the say-so of a world
not purely western less midland than swamp.
Count to infinity before garnering the legacy part fuse
part ginger melding into water. Restored dreams turn
drams while opening first-come last-served mantras.
Think of a word that starts with *o* that tips the pride

to deeper levels than old soil would give. Binding
the tops of weeds to form a better and more perfect bloom.

Crass clearing your current options make gauntlet dreamery a ledge ledger or
cellulose equator mountain into parasol. Everybody has seen the ad clothespins
interlocking on a linen banner park benches cooing observed wind speeds
shearing the yearlong memorial silos filled with timothy and sumac. Sponsor a
child and she may grow up infinitely young.

mantras for geldings
soil deep banners
begging for growth

Say you mean privation. If the beggar cased in plexiglass
is complicit with pin and hammer action reducing the world
to scrap law. Helvetica bolsters while *anti-* cloaks the base camp
bon viver. Tram runs half a mile under dynamites its clothing
narrow bodies trip over one another unearth *opulence* from synergies
deemed by their "spade and trowel" pseudonym. Dichromatic
net worth: it isn't appropriate yet for facts but their correlates
joke at our expense an underclass human kind of well *I grapple*
with that earring she lost down the disposal her secret leaked.

Welcome home face of my type. The row of homes dons nimble facts and frames
what they aspire to free. Correlatives appear old friends even when disposed.
The dream deposed was I resistant to all but what was literal leaking zilch. A
breath is but a chromatic away from dissolution of impending underclassmen run
through folly.

> patched caves yawn
> granular *touché* blown
> far beyond chatter

Acts of error wither. Being predisposed to opt out
of the synergies. Courier New reverts to scrap secretion.
Plenary trams run pseudo code from here to
everywhere. Meet me at the office of endowment plenty
of spade work to be undertaken. Class issues act as
dynamite still pinned to hammers drowning in
accidental leakage. The river is a gauche investment
in begging glassy-eyed and bowled over by the word.

By the way remember to remain endorsed by endings.

Signatory I try hashing some sense into face time. Stash the bones climbed juxtaposed class reunion. Brightest cove graduate you have miles to glide lower. Goodbye kilns heat the reveler to inebriation. Put the olive branch to venerable morning hello through milkweb and static cling. We have already established ourselves in conversation.

> owls work errors
> in peace scrap
> pinned sleet vestments

Put your nose to the anchor freeze the needle. Shortages will
purge themselves of choice. Sacks of jade will feather seeing.
Angles lop off heights hair styles bound in name only.
The exquisite planets reign (rain) in a pitch (evaporate).
Nurses clip their charts wipe screens prepare the butcher's block
swath it in aloe. Isis errs without object opens
the refrigerator door notices blinks. There you are. *There.*
A candidate for apocalypse staring at the leak and so we use
payback as drill bit at the fingertips the teeth. The drink sours.

Active parades deflect the rain or is error the opposite of mourning? Links to sprinkle do not a sheaf of water make. *How to sleep* is selling high. Objections come to seem objectives here in the environment of a candidate unblessed by thrumming sours. Fill dirt is the dissolution of choice. Ones stares at what is gapping high and pours away the drink.

> wedding invitation our
> never satisfied calypso
> injury divides beat

Store your poise. I whiten when I anger. Gap up scrap the
weeping and let go and mind greases adhere to town-maker
act particularly cool but nicely bash the water lily boyish flats can't
keep track of high dive fear. Reinstall pay half-attention. Your
shin splint drips up-braided. Park scrounges when environs give out.
Price is price. There's drama an approach a taste to ointment.
A plus sign smart toughens the take swells the competitive
search and swaps couch for macramé. Dishonesty dates the power
coining folk. Bleat of diffident soil — go long. This catches all.

One hitch: the door one might have kept safe from the icicles is firmly exquisitely shut. Now notices in the places planets are. The heart follows eyeliner objecting to wallowing although no solution seems wiped from the lip synch of performance. Needling will have been no one's hobby when the shortages are brought to light on shining screens.

reason leaves crumbs
unless dyspepsia endures
cool heart contracts

A candidate seen wallowing in rain repairs to the charts.
Errors make the madrigal. Doors listening lead to
the obvious. Notice heights and how they make you feel.
A hair style indicative of brinkmanship allows for afterward.
This hitching to purgation shows off vapor's fine politics.
Objections to the contrary evolution comes to seem
a choice. One lips off to the nurses then spends
a hollow lifetime in the act of making shame
a career among the waves' planetary rotunda.

Does it matter that we cater to unknown synapses the first-born nautical mile closed each month for repairs? Then takes two steps backward and waits for further instructions. Envelop me on some brink. *I find you unfeeling* removed graceful as tiny snows as central night where street blocks reflection in a painless exercise of planets' prototype.

always wrong about
how to get
well on material

Overthought thoughtless runs out. Contraption is
contradictory thus we get blamed for what is not ours
to watch an accident occur and doubt the cerebral juju.
Damned if on the other station handing over *achtung*
suspends dis- ah there it goes! Without seeding the scope of it
edge listens very long to their solicitous lows howitzers of twirl
figure eights iodine RPMs cover sheet calibrations. I see horizons
amounting. Weakened avatars a lively outlet "troubles" perhaps.
Steep. To get even hike down palms burning. To ask for her.

Revolutions per menagerie weakness trotted out as explanation for the troubling cerebellum. Eight might seem elite but it is painful watching stars go down. This lame game damning rapture for the level that it is. Getting to psalms means doubt without elastic and the jitters all in one fell accident. *Roger* says the machine pressing into you.

> rap with dissonance
> palms stretched outward
> trouble from stars

Prince of pretext weakens argument a little wall provided
for the sake of clanking via copter above all the space
that covers neighborhoods. Gut lines slow the quiver
of the tall tone. Low-down is like sugar never quiet
enough. The salt content of what we buy has fallen from
the level where we calibrated a lame recipe opposed to
the reciprocal steep shelving of a winter mile construed
of sheer will built into persistence. One gets even in one's dream
still thoughtlessly with diction partway yearning.

Today there is a peace *copies* the movable blackwood barriers so calm that the mind elevates eclectic over-the-top offers: how did you do that? You enjoy the inn you rue. To run away together I think what you want is an investigation without borders the defamed landscape. Eden-swap a people at play with the portable asterisk the star frost of *maybe*.

> licentious clarion banquet
> integral subway contribution
> true of love

Additive sect prances and postures a minor protuberance
shot from way back when. In the theater scarfing twin row homes
meet broken second city where tricks flay inevitable sweet
as diamond bat-around salubrious toast glasses flaring
hellward plug's layout policy set in potable sodium. Savant
sockets intone a bingo spread five across. *Are you haunting me
for the lack of anything?* Night has a shelf life we appear obese to
tilted one side over par. So little to do with suffering part attribute
part ingredient's common base droning on about the year.

Ace reporter reads the haunt around hen homes. Tributaries mean moist hype. And then a little lobby re-appears to form a sect that will atone for flyers left on doors. Are you lugging bingo hardware to the night life we encompass? Why or why not? Rickety playthings make for low-grade bonding far from flinging suffering to base.

playout practice policy
in drone line
waiting for peace

Telltale retreats imbue biology with furniture. Venting the heat
with certainty bears repeating. The lingo passes for a sense of *glide*
as sodium appears read into diets plus fluff. Gradations of the obvious
condone varieties of diamonds for the crosswords and acrostic
machinations. Lacking theater the firm moves toward then
the clock shows signs of giving out one toasts something.
Pockets of tilt seem to bemoan revered and yearlong
devastation much like hell intoned in the recesses. All night
the riled birds divvy up sounds floating in the public domain.

The firm is cobbled from kite string and sandwich wrappers dawdling headlines
guests or enemies wait for you to loosen up arguing whether or not there exists a
blood in each small decision propped up fin upstaging echo. The firm is like that
casket of a thousand varietals spouting chatter against manicures which keep you
shell-shocked tight-lipped.

grubs born in
hands-free rainbows
total pitch count

The autopsy conducted under handcrafted suction is the sheaf
of a working hour. The meek shall bear down sling anathemas
at allegory. Sandbox binds clocks in. The firm moves emptiness
out of direct mouth-to-wrist contact. Puckers and closes on your
carnivorous recollection. If the sea is searching for machine-minted
epistles the speech it delivers is too simple. A starfish taboo must
slip forget groan for you will rarely pay it a compliment despite
forced feeding. A year hidden from coves of allographic wind
slaps birds against sheetrock aboriginal yellows against summit.

Inspect firm emptiness then speak. Akimbo policies numb the gathered view of
carnage. Known epistolary strolls through splintered sheetrock bring to mind
these cloves of simple. Blind young speech affords no box of sand. A sea bathed

year of clocks will close off recollection. There are payments that confound the yield of working for a feeble hour.

> loose clocks override
> kin bathing repeat
> signs allopathic sea

If compromise is duck soup newly minted jam replies to speech
alongside homonyms that spar with partnering apostrophes.
Hidden wind betrays the coloration of land loss. And the constant sea
inspires down vests to cover craft and fault line. Simple rules apply
to roan as to monopolies. The yellow tones detain the eye.
Forgetful mornings follow sleep-filled nights clocking straight-line
lyrics mouthed by lay person wristbands feature mantras rendered
lines to say against the recollected shells that wash forth
then slip back with slap song into acres of unboxed white.

They flit away unbeknownst to us turn fading on its back. And while I might
walk my apocryphal Ts into gentle glower burrow borrow— so many variations.
X marks the marriage to scratch rush hour splurges at stop's deduction runs
aground. Clocktrace rehearses (what one *g* would intrude on) the refinery counts
to ten then shuts out sky.

feasting on prolific
rockfish dunes exploit
her tragic laugh

Most compressions yield promising homilies. Not today's events.
Visualize partnering with the Orient. Punctuate mislabeled jars
the songside of what happens conspirator or lamb: it takes a village.
Silver-plated and scoffed at dunked in wastefulness. Don't scratch
if you must raft to the end of creation (as though rashes invest their
agita in monopolistic no-bid romance). *Smile please.* Propose to her
by land line water's retreat. Guess who's late again. Theirs to colorize
squelch vs. lure Park Place Mt. Sinai Baltic Ave into our cloakroom
switch among predilections biases that grate us into calmer birth.

In punctuation waste turns lay-by. There's a noose to please in view of prior
sweating. The colonies are colorized with predisposed entirety to batch. When
late beats out never then you know that partnering is on some footing that will
promise noon ballistics. Templates fit the mood of scoffage. Many partings make

flight work.

> faith beast biases
> the polis east
> no end in

Label the B-side polis. Dribs and drabs of proof will cinch corsets
and singe the test case smoothing through full *cirque de pluie.* Imagine
swearing in a fool and failing to step in. Caloric windfall's only tepid
if you make it so. Recreation trims the roomful of predictions. Home
sweet happenstance and such. Lamb bake's not the same as rum cake
and the brats go home with abductors. If I smile will you promise to
clip shoulder-length loquacity? Impress or keep those guesses
to yourself. Lure me to St. Louis and produce a bell full
of dark brass consistent with some seasonal purebred.

Beyond the anise music in water. Such is shoulder's light the sweated muzak a la
sophomoric ruffling. Truest display not knowing whether dawn will condescend
the process of a novel soul *you;* or *sol* as in medicinal circles they gossip about
diagnosis pipeline astronautics and method's metric. Grab on and don't let go
these hostage links.

> fete buoys tied
> imbibe drought your
> entangled figure B

Couples do away with one another. I am off the hobby glucose-sick.
Germ's crop prevents defensive pollutants from splashing. Case in point
isn't that the heralded summary. Ready for *pluribus*: labels dross
affiliate renewal as a foundation for roughhousing. A fool who persists
in the wind by any other name skims the pot persists and jabs at air.
Roll again lead me forward to your impression. Damn this notation.
Interlocute for stance has spent its revolt and labor deserves the ballroom
to itself. "Brat" (the root) undercuts chipper forecasts. The great arch
is our concretized terminal. The doll coffin looks as though it belongs.

Roll the coffers here this burly spring when voltage lifts and everything's
inductive. Take your turn at proving we transcend notation by mere slink of
feathered petals and root hairs drawing down the bed of sky. Line item obvious it
was put to stray while the corn grows to their fence lines. Thus do some of us
proceed to play our role of privilege.

ballroom chafes night
air if chipped
dolls appear burlesque

Fences are for neighbors absent supervision. Coffers fill to blinking
without hesitation. Crisp enumerators house themselves where
roughness fends off movement. *Chip seal wants to be your
cover.* Right away rotation breeds a cupola to house the spools
of doll slips. Longing to be noticed a symptom of the forecaster
lodged too long in present tense impressing one mirror
after the next skimming another locomotive blip. Laborious
two-step paces the train into root stations where the great stance
holds to read-throughs of the picture soon finished stroke.

Fencing volume let it all drip (not rule out) the refresher course (coarsely)
conducting searches replenishes you bare. Not to be suffocated outdone by the
full nelson of cloud. This is not the confiscated implement sacred even "starry
night" as it was written for a strain of grudge or freight: *at what time did she jump?*
Sung: the noose came around.

séance rift what
volleys ebb with
joylessly clear as

Ostensibly an ocean heats up faster first among its treasured
unbounded perjuries that is if one were to excite the recuperating
breath and model detained real estate. The sealants count our deaths
and though numinous they seem petty. Accu-weather playwright
here and then our painter of futures may you descry the tingsha
domino chairs taped-off aisle a gradual smoke in which honorees
dissemble black lung persuasion as gap. Arboretum's "wow" starts
in a few seconds and the broadness of it or serpent-like as they say
when purer land catches on the felt of meadows bolt to bone.

Ann Arbor latches onto cups along the aisle. Not far away are meadows. Fair
market signs divide the quad where branch by branch this spring the ceaseless
tones of birds become a cloth of music. One may dabble in sonorities while others
read. Headphones guarantee the loss of natural music that never will recuperate
from designated driving.

absconding with tincture

                              voracious fire mead
                              thrashes in head

Pedestals crowd up with goodness of fit. The lush gum trees
grow latched to meadow lines. A future mockingbird may leave us
whistling in the aisles. Juried posture leaves detainees safe
within their cells to be observed then not observed then
vanished. Is an ocean a *for sure* thing? Romance languages
by custom remain warm as they are gradual in brushing inner
life. The honor of performing breaks into common speech
when breath is the dependable component of an evening.
We share too few exits in our cocktail hours.

At odds they lived a while on Gardner Island poked at voids quicksand
fragmentary capes torn loose from continental shoelace consummated by green
tropic. Waistdeep we almost made it out alive yes from sleep. Desolate emblem
tinnitus campfire biped sapien survival. You're getting warmer colder on
purpose waving at the giant petrels.

                              wheel escalates fledgling
                              go-seek where light
                              wedges in tread

There's the gum of mind happy median aborted from *objet d'une
passion.* Tempered display case break-in the final tweet hooting
and booing. Subtitled mock trial that you might do time by so what
then forget it . . . Set the alarm before leaving your shifting wardrobe.
Accept your conviction *ferveur* that domes grow permanent with
eschew bleaching cure the new century by veto depose its former
trip advisor chairperson of all subtle interiors. It's a bargaining chip
often turned in declared customary a mawkish CPR or new line
of languor baja of complexes padding the middle with nonsense.

Levitate this minor century past its broth. Break into wardrobe by way of a Venn
diagram in the hope of showing common interiors. Chips tending to be down
may populate the optics of alarm braving impending trials through visualization
as technique. The vault is where our fire is kept apart from elemental scurrying.
In the bargain a certificate is chalk.

beneath rescuing in
a minor key

alarm breaks ranks

Boo took away our breath and then the century flipped over. Sense
brought home some of itself before the custom shifted to distemper.
Displays of hope made padlocks seal the middling interiors
with chairs placed in broad rows as if to fend off chaos.
Subtlety looked numb having ripped live domes away.
As usual bleach ran in short supply. Non sequiturs moved languor
to a different disposition ramping up the semblance
in dizzy flame. To bargain seemed equal to fretting through
the flight without the honeybees inhaling all the good in posies.

Postcards offer mint. In relative calm day prices escape too high. Your laced
genes charge more for prowl and lip. We pay for body twice eggs transferred
from spoon to slower arc. Crack open datebook where power adapts articulation
to combine. Ghosts expel non-being vita in cognito an alphabet scripted on black
rock shut-eye composure.

> stood up again
> fluorite shell nebulized
> industriously longing for

I was caught underneath unaware that sarc had a bite to it.
Any poppy field will dwindle. To make time one must work
in layers un-ply the gate which procreates well wreaking and inferior
after said incubation said soirée. Post-rhyme rowed into non-neighborly
realms ducking without cover tearing the roof off someone's wintry circle.
Oh but the rains reflect sequestered softeners their rinse cycles seasonal
subtractions grief. As always indicates you can't feel altered unless
your feet or knees or collar bone exempt another expectant mouth.
Flames honey against gnats. Disparate rayon courts chaos marries it.

Are there views from rooftops one can name beyond the rhyme? Neighbors leaf
through questions and then grieve discovery post-flames. Our procreative
nightmare fosters edgy clothes to follow incubation deemed sacred post-soirée.
Many hearts have been defined by gates. Home life is in there where being alone
guarantees a lifetime of just that.

> winter proves hypothetical
> innocence altered once
> restores the grieving

146

What is softer than grief? Not another mouth to feed and equally
no rhyme that sows new patterns into brain fire. Making time appear
to last is poppycock. Subtraction holds the key to understanding
what has frosted over pliant rains. Our yard is made of bone.
Sunlight feeds live ones a substance to fuel courting. Flecked
divans start to feel like granite although rayon would be closer
to embedded torque. I thrill therefore I rearrange what comprises
ambience. Is sarcasm elastic? Doubt takes wheels and you show
a unique ability to spin them one concurrent with the rest.

Creatureless above. Just try centering the track icy quintuplet treacherous as view
from over there. The distant three-inch skin a game extrudes a self braced for
noctus hearts sounding out their supra-rational noise do not catch on. Oracular
hatches and breeds better to be fooled with you suppose than turned against the
premise to be gutted.

> tourniquet dictionary ingests
> revolutions per montage
> one needs proof

In the beginning sadness sows understanding. Mental fire
takes wheels a unique head-against-stall-door relapse. We thrill
into new fuel where divans like elastic yards have over-rained
tongue's substance. I rearrange spin last first-in-rhyme courting
candid shots you serve concurrently. Ability comprises another bone
patterned after time. Granite key subtracts embedded shrinkwrap.
In the presentation nutrient nourishes surprise intuits abreactive
trot until *am* no longer pushes back. Object floats as blotter.
Diver dredges the versatile crevices of black book oceans.

Range of motion yields to nourishment in absentia. Lack of object plenary
patterns run-throughs of the dark side not composed. A minute more and black
endures being despair. The cast of thou/sand patterns riffs upon the omniplex of
spin fields. Lumens come to papa before dying to the wall. As if to mitigate the
lapse of resources toward a blotter.

soften relapse often
nutrients from crevices
source versatile darkness

Stretch shot amounts to traction. Watch the sinister refract.

A lot of acting out substantiates the pins gone down because
perhaps they're never limber. We on divans last. Rills live in
the mind. Mentation doubts lush fields though watered;
many nutrients afford our intuition. Water lifts. Its edges
hold concurrent rain. Is ability cast in color yet? If I am
to be objective who's your patter(n)? Verses till the sealed
test. Lacking looks the seams give way to spun things.
Servant leadership remains a gift of tongues not spoken.

Estranged from any motive that is not this side of Syd. That adios stare call it
glance and menses a cohabitation of bus fume omega mineral male / female
petroglyph. Opine as to which castaway the *pre* of concept archaic cloth. Did she
mention you wouldn't flirt with the world that came to collect its desperate chaff.
Gain footing on forgiving walls.

> a molar in
> the fist is
> worth two flaws

The impossible: here you could expand on bulldozed hydrangeas
for strike/spare combinations lanes we digress by. *Sicitur ad astra*
thus we proceed assume the record wring bleach from twigs
paper and scissors paraphernalia undershirt rags. Our receipts are
voided in office parks chewable pills the handset replaces saki
teacup and mortar gelatinous freckled. Ability is abuse clear as
whatever you might think well of impounds the aforementioned
sluice. Menstrual sky spoons us lower. Rotary caste raked over towels.
Calamine-dizzy from the pat on your back urges you to quit at five of five.

Strike two for saki. Blanch under the weight of clarity as if playing the spoons
were placating compound. Rotary phones tempt undershirts to breathe
paraphernalia into scissor range. The mortar pests the chewable vials the freckled
ditzy quit-course deigning to be five of this assumed of that and always voided
by gelatinous bay mend.

> mensa plants spoon
> saki across pounds
> undershirt and paraphernalia

Camiseta meaning t-shirt owns a little fragrance past the fact
of what the word might mean. *And if you know teach me to read.*

Ability looms over primalcast. What I cannot manage won't exist
apart from the gelatinous abuse blackened by depression. Why not
scissor out the person in the photograph who took away the consecrated pills
and ate them right in front of you? Whose off-shore mood are we
permitting now? Paraphernalia runs majority opinion ragged
for it's raging in the layers that precede us. Thinking is a gift
and scourge as dizzy as all summer playing spoons for the sensation.

Camisole sense-memory. Scranton branch snaps whip and cubistry climbs down
at dawn because we were scorched once with rumor a sliderule sun/cloud
consistency reaping what you bury analyzed tom-tom brattle in essence crowning
you with nightsweat simulcast. Vision: you may enter the parallel that saints dig
out for real for us *go under.*

> she missed an
> edge walking it
> back to Act

*III. Stage left. Window trapping the crisscrossed power lines godlets over mouths like
orphic tape recorders back to the same. Repeat. Candid's okay to be intrigued as a
transition human breath snuck in between grooveless maturation. Syd and Eechee rest
their waning grins on abysmal rocking chairs on lily-white porticos. A fire rises then*

S: Earth steps away from you when gimlets of roofing detach the temperature
chandelier of I. Thought we were an aluminum shambles but guess what's next
among the sirenese?

E: Blanch me tremolo your laudsheep's clothier's got the better of yew; things
tangle from the quasi Lasso Apso under beamlets where old shadows purred.

S: Particular you mean blank as a judgment supposes. Disposal shadowing
buckle fathers slash deeply in sleepwalk the lunesque softheel of grasses blur blur
blur. Bleat of skinny bark the canine arcana minimus rex quantity unknown. No
end as bookend or birthmark. What way is this to unclothe the sound?

*Leans into seeps out of frees arm from elbow another burn-free flame 'changed life.' This
could be (how it IS it IS) referenced by rumbling from defensive breach betrothal butanol
breath.*

Exit.   *Entry.*

E: Exculp exclamist lowdown lunacy blurs yon bleeping. We pose what we impose struck blond in whinnying nine flays. The candidate aflame in whitelings minimaturally stoking prior wounds.

S: Blush less to begin cobalt's coagulation. Sculpt help from promontories and observation deck's reigns pulled up to your chin so the stilts crack and drag into woe-is-me borderline sing-along dishes shatter. The photomusic swings from cordoned stables. 'We' is a pain in the— You don't think twice I've noticed. Posing stops the iris dead in its scent.

E: Chintz boils down to a *vivace* and then cordons off the entryway (and by the way): *look at my pair of irises why don't you*! Vice squad wracks its collegial brain timber just about to deck the spat lines on the border's hemline.

S: You exhumed a forest so you could get at me. Control panel glitz ropes off the scene. They don't bloom nearly as well that's why and shouting will have nothing but conch pinks and lavatory violets to render and they will pattern us after chalk lines on the fertile vase and I will read an instrument's scraped off starlight as nothing grows into N-O-T-H-I-N-G murmuring to you or me:

> Downsize your assonant
> self so that
> cubbyholes may blunder
> through your adobe
> voice with ease

E: Indica-marsh too mellowy to brew. I think a hut slathered with puce would do. Some gnome mid-leased to cue us would be bellwethery hemline for the voiced allit-tone panes. Pertextative small laminates give edge to what is not yet known. I hear Conchita laughing now at minnows. Shelf is wrung out of the ladder stung. For slung down under into twelve or so dis-Jungs.

S: Paella and guitar cut with starfruit suggests distraught Friday night openings dolorous straw. Go climb la niña esta noche . . . cracked mill gives ground a quarter mile up carried into agnostic banter as weather struggles out. Bristles a place to keep your crown and title and virgin cantos. Maman memorized . . . yet I trail. Finish the

> crux leashed to bell
> and pier's bracket
> driven wobbly

until blackout bends tune into close alignment.

E: This paso doble leaves the miles in tight quarters. Listen to the wharf turn dreamed niña's lithe *cantadas* into wild minutiae mutually frayed yet sweet. The leashes to which I subscribe the wobbly pier the rucksacks lodged in moldy books. As pleated sanguine lift-off breathes the day.

S: You claim to forget buena vista where shipwrecks huddle together at syllabus level portals thrown wide. Murcia for mercy extremadura for impresario. I've seen you adopt a child of variants lashes masking "the dip" all nakedness aside the choreography of your lost *bodas de sangre* fowl whose blithe waters part like gauze sails among late afternoon sunrises.

E: Lullaby holds steady breath within speakeasy of the moon. Despair endowed with flash contagion trances all the little blithedom with its curse a fabric matching once the drawn cloud curtains. Harshening as rash the simple facets of mid-day where I am trilling syllables of *regresar* and merciful owl tones reach the inner ear near visages. *Juntos por favor.* All wanting is the shimmy of simplicity's inversion traced from you.

S: All or none? One isolate lake or pyramid and its denuded rectangles of fire digestible trinkets that cymbals inhere to these small sounds you and I our churlish acts— they whorl in and out side to saddle. Factorial wests scarps that many compile our starving

I

sparrow or blackbird

holiday or trembling

exodus of *alma* and mooncrest broken limestone trickling onto flat sunlit drapes. These are our common rooms los duendes de fastidio. Shroud drawn over Madre y Maman and parlor (pallor?) of glimmer.

E: *Parler?* Askance atrance and fact pared into thirds to wake toward the pile of stars. If saddle westing toward yes plants dried

and lacking as we are

at rest sierra

look qua si

pressed limn touched treacle of vast low kindred warm tones husky red to blue tended and

water is the carapace
protective toward thee
and what is thine
in lust once muscled carved.

S: Some central river thought this heard you oiling horizons so here. Take it.
What caves away from musculature one ample nostrum of twill at a time.
To appall the leathered roots she strokes their finer sins of witness quatrained
nightstand transitives outbreathings standing up against stain wiry tears gone
perilously dark . . . and so if we touch bottom again we are owned and
underwritten by sick conditionals . . . and if we build back to stammer and
smother the illuminated body acting as skyline

figuratively unfulfilled
these Adriatic zeros
extinguished flint
it cannot say what it wants!

                                    You unknow yourself and that's about moving up down
and
                          over straw sawdust cholera

E: Underscore the rivulet de-plays gravity. Each figure minus taken-back words.
Ample with nuisance wind. To stamina each flotilla glows neonish in some tacit
mind-owned witness. Palpatetic parapluie yet starched flint-like as touché barbs
inner nexus *yes*.

                                        Shaft the cumulative
                                        oiling of a platelet
                                        how(ever) young
                                        do you envision you
                                        would grow to be
                                        (to seem)?

 S: Your stutter-step stream from posh footholds and mouth forms / discards clay
from desert spires fast-forwards the movement of coal through furrow and praxis
the living welt *dust tumbles* papercut seeds excavate image around briar and sash
leap like adoring masses— again we imitate circuits nothing too crushed that it
couldn't make up a parable cabal-flower jupiter shadow *jouissance* in surround as
if it were a criminal act *the whisper of dust* Let's accumulate solitudes through
webbing and vestibules append eyesight if it okays the fleet follows obedient

palpitation hull fashioned from wicker *the sweeping terrarium of middles* ditto ergo sum—

A robin under cloak of euphemism announces Syd in her presence be unafraid of the human hi-lo hallowed like halo settled in for the centipedal year. Eechee branches her arms toward voice and holds threads of vibrato as thought silvers to her basking in the juntos rush.

E: Wake to spritz of newbirds stippling toward legato in neglect of fossil fuel. A planet tugs at an oncoming madrigal dressed in perfect weave. The lashes craft new eyesight. Circuitry concedes to ambidextrous sprint lines into wheel light posh as leash lamps posing near the nest. Away shrill icelets then the yield of narrow warmth about to tether joy to breast. Wallow of nouns cheat purity of thought unless impending brevity

> sum of least . . . or is it
> yon risotto eminence
> qua prana bounced
> from you
> solo middling
> in the lull of terra
> firma trained to seem
> true vestibule

S: Cut out early then dial a truer room—*all of it whispers a slight whistle an easy almost granted you versus you departing*

> arpeggio
> up to waist
>   acci-dent
> hub of night more night than
>   mattress musk   *ahhh* burlap
>   illusion   troupe

Upperworld don't look back for me. As I rock in my ellipse break out of causeway shuttle woven tightly around turgid formula and borax white feet. See me stretch this orbit this tag-along limp. *Poor little strangeness* you and your idyllic pageant mounting staff to scantly clothed tablet. Drop in on eidolon your ripple growing multiple thirsts thrashes where we applaud late shadow's arithmetic

                    wade back into
                    skelter *opus*
                    contra naturalis
                    dual dos duet
                    twice as tandem
                    bound by vines infirm

matte red among bloat and rudder. Riches pinned to one-way window flag of
run-on glass multi-handed (headed?) posthumous rhyme is a crumb sentence
distended against earth not the same as you

                    beginning to wade
                    through dominus
                    ravine energism

Acted upon. The hush of one another so hand to hand a curt 'may we all rise.'
Convenience of an approximate circle. His and hers. Together: "Long ago if I remember
rightly my life was . . .un festin . . . Tu resteras hyène"

            (you shall remain)   *Tersely*

                    & by order of the City of prodigals
                    joined as

Arithmetic endures the brain that houses its conception.
Rings around prospective levitation draw thought
upward into lucid poses. Under the aegis of determinism
one releases separation from companionable anxiety.
A truce reforms the formulaic imposition to resemble
the idea of *whose long legs* depicting distance
to and from the partial scales in a harmonic
minor key. The lips pursed defer to inner patterns
that turn present tense into a minaret from recollection.

What is to pass equally will happen. Pursed fact parses the impartial prepositions
that determine how the felt momentum is originally comprised merely of
moments. A vault of quizzical responses underlies the place of prayer by accident
or by design. Harmony works like that enduring pose layered in multiples held
down in brains still various.

scales held long

in multiple keys
composed from scratch

Surpassed and ticketed a tall order detains planets washed
clean except for their terror diaphanous braid your cough
interjects. Flung as far dove turned loose among rafts
compensates and gathers resolutely an impartial language
of tiredness. Parity. Legish fresh demure all these incidentals
are opposite scapegoat measurement from stud to pane lies
your lockbox boredom. Our garland will disintegrate sure as
every line in sand or carved *O* in birch consoles a cataract.
Confront a beginning scaled by crosshairs and false sightings.

You may outburst into your multivariate prisons clinks as white-gray seductions
run coast to coast. You can go and let your lover wait at the rooftop café but
there's no point in lying about the stand-off unsung precautionary tale as the self-
regulation of opposites flight plan manifest and gear of lightning leaping at the
dual desert chuparosa and lupine.

> anthem every minute
> ineluctable sigh hints
> of space shrink

Genuflecting to the thought of sightings one relents in hope
of landing proof. *This land is la la land*. Twitched gesture strains
canvas as the surface thickens. Vowels acquire perfection
in succession of cantatas. As consonantal braces fix the squares
each craft constrains defining orbits. Each member of the populace
impairs by leaving what deserves to be subtracted
in a manner tentative by sight. The senses starve us for simplicity
at stud level of the dwelling. In whose house *am safe* within
these measured lines despite the sand's arriving in rough waves.

Watch branch be thick with vowels enlisted for a wind emergency. Each new
sprint of growth draws on the atmosphere for a safe milk. Enumerated senses
clock the unrelenting life force at an orbital velocity of rough wave number.
Definition lasts about as long as the defined (victims positioned) in new casings:
trimmed possessions seen mid-flight.

> indwelling cantata safe
> against waves bracing

for planned succession

Roughness gapes at reticence rather than quiescing. We brace in pairs
for example the what-for tales time out bedtime yessed to death
beyond stranded plow and nothing but lake rain where Reichstag flood
plain bucks the seasonal chain as it straps bravo to the positioning system.
September declines cohort slips between cast and role reversal skips
the preliminary friendships the strummed gustatory crust "in whose
house" we refrained from touching bullet sashes. Flanges unscrew soul
to fulfill their flush surface rancidity periscope clean as your eyes. Delirious
one wishes domicile flagged as shingled inebriation curbs the itinerary.

Renal traffic at hourglass multiples. Every science has descriptively coded us into
milk-gray udders *dearest* sagging trunks of the elephantine readypac boasts
cigarette hum on polished optical knife-strain. Boneless girder chronicity passes
through small intestinal diploma hymns. In Latin depth is hybris waiting for the
private practice of minutes.

> hollow hollow hollow
> three strokes closer
> to the *exercitia*

Downward turns to depth fosters peri-perceptual *a la breve* immersion
in topography from strums. The placid sheet of laketop that ingests no rain
resists intrusion. Meanwhile reverence between friends rises. Motion as thought
permits a shift in roles. A giveaway means more than several relaxed chain links.
Ionesco placed change on stage perhaps in hope that knowledge might tilt
into wisdom given clarity and time. Whatever seasons are they easily
accommodate eyes fallen to rest. Lower and lower into truth one sleeps if only
to forget that in the morning domicile there are exhaust points reasons
to debrief selected state of being in the uninfected hours preceding.

Had to be propped up to reach the point of hell where charred truth had to be
tossed. Accommodations are born not made. Lenten children tap dance on the
unmarked pavement. Laudatory moonlight rinses friends after their roles right
justify new costumes. Inflammable gear resists infection and the de rigueur
infection of a strum.

gaps in topos
allow in water
and give clarity

Infection our shots rang out of upward as motive not simulacra.
Desecrated topos the logos under erroneous watch consigns long kisses
before accepting burlesque atomistic dance incentive. Backdated to this
commotion each year droops the vein we highwire walk-on whimsy with.
Feat establishes its level where pugnacious vertex captures a look. Stagnant
eyes rout modal hearts eke out incessant notices so where one endows
rest with water-wings and topical consortium a Southwest low declares itself
numbly across a neutral sea. *Spiritus asper.* Discodial (but cordial) playful insults
roam a greater Artesia gender so-totaling loss among its vacuous acquisitions.

Microphagic *siempre un* misdemeanor your head-in-the-snail routine. Hot as
qualifying blue ribbon sinecure like you attacking someone else's wrong
sleeveless muscles made wherever a sensational bombing happens the office they
occupied the marvelous game is forfeited –ly and –ive *come off it* for the copyright
is inundated by scratched typo as tip.

> stopwatch irruption why
> larval dregs book
> a wedding venue

Reaction: airy backwash. *Nunca* cessation topical or other(wise). Is suicide
logostomy? Where on the compass does a vein leave off? One notices and one
forgets (what does that equal). Quashage? Now is the time for neural norms
to have been fitted for heartfelt subtraction. What is the difference between
real property and your vast imagination? *Give me numbers when you speak
of hell and motion thickness.* The tropics might some day include you. A high
wire act proved silence correlates with mascara. That's *subtle* with a capital *b.*
Sure let's go out some time to test our wings (to taste) the fruits of
consolidation where the consolation prize left off hemorrhaging discord.

It's not all in the wrist whispered the protagonist of high wire (t)act. Mascara
planes the sightline of the echo-eyes. Redeeming plenary fault lines from their
real inert propitious largo wingspan hologram. *Most employees pace* at liberty but
not at leisure. The fruits of staying-in can be dissolved as fast as feeling in your
heart a full unplanned subtraction.

> thick veils unwash
> window clarity prized
> noticed only now

Shoulder-fired and glinting glazed wanders the moistness of *homopterous cilia* flirting with another name as known the shakiest part of the northern lights. Our earned gulfs board polarized windows its dyads of uranium and seesaw patterns cave-dry skin abruptly a port of call for tutelage. Mosses reflect glass dunes at near tide pointing devices wasp stripes the undersense a figure of pinpoint dabs (solid light) a yard between does not recognize the invisibles but was told to wait for further instruments of rain. Make sure that what you make is sure or else if there are no more exams save for phonetical engorgement the booklet garnished with ballistic shock Etymon's presence is a lonely revolving condition.

Pawn *he who closes the door* bait for a loophole. I am a strangeness or a moral person per sound through mask slit. Tell the tunnel to tell the truth at its dismissal. *Imagines et lares* intentional press recants admission prevailing wind for obvious puffed up thespian rattles its double-sheeted don't quote. Whatever is orangeclad cannot interact with comeback.

> lapis totem bland
> say can you
> lazuli as *religio*

Whatever is in hock diminishes the fundament. An overload self-painted with the rain with flavored name between making and polarities. How to stay attuned considering proliferation of invisibles. Examination never can encompass conscience. Shock as daily fare makes tempering a constant. Pinpointing on a stray map remains insufficient. The tide's inside us. No curve to infinity can mimic bells. The lights go south. There is a yard of solid flight turned pale. An indivisible haze thickens. What one learns tilts just beneath pretend concern. Selves so small they charm their matching minds to proclaim caves yards requiring glass. Moments at a time there is no way to play the clock. To measure yourself yields full interference with the slaving.

Point to pins for puncture of redundancy. Divide by glass. At the time a moment passes what else leaves the fund? Yield tilts toward flesh and leaving won't decide. In stride go stray splinters of certitude in name only minions left in hock. If there are compasses available for distribution sign the tide-man. Sign the selfsame. Sign the clock.

shells mimic bells
redundantly tilt toward
this latent wind

In-crowd chooses where and when words similar to regurge and backstop may result. Lime ridge and orange rind scents the irregularity a veiled disguise. What else reigns over ruckus does not order *via regia* the towers' depth nor hears its factious pleas. Orchid radios rake coals while they breathe out noetic assemblage. Marooned never mind means scarce but don't rely on sound. Infighting seethes in its natural cause. Personified dayslope's unexplained inclusion triggers happiness hounding godmother beginnings until they match basilica. That may be all creation has written for its reunion its pardon me cult rarely a 1st edition drugged library immolates afterbath carbon slips hammers out a vivid proxy that wasn't first approved by lax shapes echoing thin.

[Clerical omission]. Go forward three spaces. Pay the guard a smile for there is absolutely nothing further from the prosecution at the gate. Order form burnout— titrate the pretense shrug it off as if you want some humanness to things. Path has *at* centrally located on lugubrious rims betting on a thin method of proof *p'o* or *kuei* finds the *yin* (she) as lasso.

> filial percept why
> nothing else comes
> home as dry

Back when there were runes to throw the candle slipped one night.
Sound rhymes with *wound* sometimes. Cult forecasts bring together differentials as proclaimed diversity as if a bull's-eye had at last been pierced. Infighting in agreement with blind diversity. A rush of force distinguished from belief asymptomatic as brushed nickel viewed in depth. Perception is a shrug. Such flight risk brings the null set close to echoic young thunder. When I cross out what I wrote ensuing ruckus paints the precipice
the color beige instead of passion paint.

Whosoever rides the posse pale into the night erodes our thinking.
Flaxseed keeps the life force regal toward creation as collective noun.
Infantile projections *leave the precipice to us.* Andante figures prominently in the contact with these echoed rungs. Timpani prolong vibrating lodged in the soft tissue. Pieced together thinking brushes depth with nickel plating. Touching upon palatable thunder amid acreage pressed to the null set encompassing granules of this sturdy flax.

> surface paint obscures
> granules beneath andante
> soft tissue sing-along

Stodgy grist meandering tapers off. Mutual and mute grips enclave to country about face coldly fantastic in line to peak. Corner office with cottered rots slowing spurns its width. Echelon's risk every puissant *s* is a distraction to the side pain vault or bronzing cloth whipped bitter reddish-black promise at its fireproof mention. Vow called off trapeze is less an -ism than the crackle of bales sacrosanct plants dipped in cacao slick as shale brotherhoods. So protect yourself for home is elsewhere chasm's resort shoved offshore said who? Rig degenerates alongside *refrigerium* hottest fungi deeply asleep— when I cross into what I spoke— targeting bulwark for horseplay this stable complex muzzled in lottery froze faster than night could catch its other knowing safe among its chorus.

Bang your head on that portent the carrier of gifts wham as compunction acts above being the felt name for the bridge to— can't get It out of Where. Upstairs as aerosol offers a handshake (no strings) attached for clean-up glass is a danger *see* if theory must tinker with the thermostat tell no one that each bulb blowing out resembles a daisy.

> patent yellows lowing
> *goodbye grass goodbye*
> fed heavyset embolism

Clots portend fossils. Racking up a look-back twice or more. Platelets thus and so until the spare sore prompts a cackle from pressed flesh. The volley of prolific fire descends upon the various. Where amid the scratch of letters on a place do bales of sanctity go by. Whosoever kindles hoods bequeaths to borderlines the standards. Home is up for generations to apply. A muzzle seems a premised keepsake. Corners we occupy proof drafts of us. First person plural tampers with the solitude each covets. Whose rig can drag possessions that belong to safety? Firewalls bristle against bleached infusion. Left beyond the opposite of right. Soft earth yields soft life requiring not a whit of combing. *When the other spoke there was a chiseling beneath.*

Chisels come in six-packs. Braced with firewall grist sans kindling. Attention paid to septic things borders on generation therapy. The safest place is (not) under the mattress where tresses and proofs of posses qua possessions hold true to sessions left behind. *In a little while the thing you cling to out of habit will evolve into a gift by going away.*

bales prompt sessions
muzzle needling left
to border proof

Stent triangulates black-on-white overlay while bridges acting as cairns neglect our take-home parables. Supposing aggression does not comp the golden rule with rings then applause is ridiculous as a hyphen the lain-to-rest whirl your stale assignment orphically wades through (microfiche bog). Who gets this will wake up and walk the plaited streak shake off space where dye is primed. In appeal convective tributes a roundness owning up to crane technique not *plumet*. Skylight nausea digs its tagline burrows. Hook grapples with references folded pressed gentle cottons contrast lint with metal wickets replacement fibers mollified and bedaubed as crossing guard signs tense against northerlies come down a notch a winged configuration she first adheres to.

If angels take revenge backwards holotypic falling down on songs already forgiven after consequent brides forge mallets a forest speech and you know how being cleared of charges can emasculate the quirk. Truantly they meander back as mendicants chalk their voices made equal parts hapless *quarrel* the cues that stitch the chest wound shut.

> closed early in
> the evening this
> wish will pigment

If we are to tinker with another side a primal dye cut must be fired. Hologrammatic windfall trumps your bag of cache. Vindication's kind of plumping our already good good fortune. Mental widgetry convalesces in atonal mass (grave) situation. What configuration trances blink? First called then dug in then molten fiche after the roast. If anyone would plait the tresses we would be endorsed for cotton wings that gentle their way southerly. Whose filters match the butterflies of northerly precaution? Whims of ivy just(ice) us and metal frenzy follows. On a good day swirl is copious astride stale precipice where cranial-sacral liftoff is applied. A comprehensive study of terrain means burrowing into tendencies with grappling antithetical to rest.

Treble butterflies define caution least cauterized among the cotton gentry in holy solo speech. A molten under-frenzy screeches underneath the thesis of a northerly terrain. Minced *palabras* still mean what tendencies sans prompting mean. Atonally invasive of the painted whole by way of metal cache. Trump card turned insidious at each sighting.

> iced wingspan offers
> legato sightings triple

Sublux nervosa where fluorescent bulbs bend down and flicker randomly against winsome inference a story about neck-in-neck autism flowering its verbs cabinets theraflux thorn bushes in comment-kitchens after everyone has put themselves down for the night. How it deforms after staring is anyone's trust to knock a rafter or a beam or a stilt out from under ones attic where one is made of cane sugar and photons and downfall. He who questions the answer that commands itself to heel *good boy good girl good without bookends*— oo essence pulp joist. Spherical metadata travels alternate routes twice turning down the volume on enriched blastulas gorging on wheat in which trochlear and abducens implicate alphabet lava and knitting dialectics after siesta.

What is the difference between *sombra* and lightning that criticizes the gorgeous fen other than breakdown swinging out over break-up. Own worst enemy turns its ire on harplife (medium-low) when there's little more than engine pointer the exfoliant stride its fructal doors left watered as cracked ice plums growing loose their *hallo* sounding out.

> blood gold or
> hobby horse winks
> supernova adoption rhetoric

Strobe splinters reverse-mend a split sky. What is the difference between foster home and sugar cane? Each downfall following the pheromones induces breathalyzed behavior. Zones hover behind definitions of the essence.
Semispherical arrangements form a cup to fill.
Transduction imitates initial instances of kitchen jousting.
Kickstands just beyond the window confirm one's worse suspension.
Is the volume up for grabs or simply as a reflex? Good for the hood and spurned by the cementric la-da of each curfew dust. Enrichment is a hobby not a life. Why not alphabetize the contents of incoming lava as it balloons into forensic taste? The situation room is full of kings who barely recognize themselves.

Siempre cement's not up for grabs (because because) balloons s/oar above the fostering. The definition of a curfew stays acrimp. Reflexively we penalize via diminuendo hobby *amateur* and lust instead for crusted stance. A downfall differs from a downpour piercing where mere moistening would cast the pheromonal essentials long as shadows.

always alpha imitating

life's worst suspicion
resisting situation rooms

You've got it backwards free beds meaning gaps leeway or the overcrowded foot march of rehearsed lilies and concerto lines. Nothing says I love you like lines diffident mobile diagram spelling out honeybee collapse. A plundered bouquet's dashed emission test— walk straight now bend over now touch your cup to the inner canal and bike path. Transduce the moister damage your incurable headache begins handheld along the below and above the beside. Spangled we ditch the dark to her aggregated standpoint. Stance dusts for fingerprints and bags a tooth cools a crawlspace boardroom axe. Detained for questioning a voluptuous fountain of *papeles* (plagues) overtake the bar component. Sambuca lotuses hang from taps like crude bells ingrained.

All too well thought-out and not enough commiserating has gone on long enough. Rebuff what's coming potentate of providence tinkertoy expertise agrees: The Greatest Show on palindrome fringe and sponge pool of cloudiness impinges wildly. Add the oriole garland to the ceiling's yammering figure with its sack of spoiled grapes and sweet rum cravats.

> tell-all excalibration never
> unjust as deity
> discourse follows suit

Brillo on the surface is unnecessary roughness. Subtract the taint of flowers at the edge of dress. A mobile unit held together with duct tape roams the woods where homes are sprinkled amid rinsed and cooling trees. *Who wants toffee?* Fingerprints of aggregated assault conform to an intended art. *I will entertain a motion to extend an offer to the concierge.* This board room needs a nanny. Bag the plexiglass: let's get some walnut in here to darken things down. *And if the room won't pop* we'll find another purpose for these letters on the door. A standpoint is an anatomical impossibility *capisce?* Most stenographers before you will have fallen to their sostenuto. Each reputation fills the vacuum claimed by advocates. A game face may be included in the RFP. Stay tuned.

Most vacuum results from oncoming addiction. *Write that down.* Whose fingerprints are on these flowers? The mobile in the room commences to compete with the invisible buffalo. I mean elephant unseen. Exaggeration's not my principal endorphin. Reputation pleads the fifth and then some musical notation taints the white with crimson a la carte.

                              quiet the point
                              tender cool through
                              trees while fallen

Every p.m./posthumous revue paraplegic ain't slangs the next best jolt *deus*
absconditis through breakwater gripe a scurvy of grade's black swan
beautification and haircut warmth begs RF signal the siren her underhanded
under/stood wave her foundling trail of Saltine pearls (can't do without). Bella
casa as toecurl limits this changeful garden. Practical accidents deter while knife-
in-the-side pins contrite visitor hours to room's dumb squint battery warning a
fluoridated love note from *moi*. Hey is grief so did you feel slighted or less alive?
Best Of memorials translate fog bank tea parties into girlish guardrail tricks. *And*
if the room won't populate undying dissertated decency . . .
Facing the scrabble of glass houses with sod farms go blind as Sterno-lit bluffs.

Into the weekend (weakening) can you send the next home for denouement a
drawn-and-quartered scenario for there are no more pure preserves left in the
unworkable clay. At the cow-horns principle eye irritant. Fireplace is a soothing
heroine of ash and homelife. Outlets glower at headlight scratched blown fuse
salutes somewhere a city trembles.

femme á homme
stairs we transcribe
rush through quaternity

4.

fore(fold) winter
shields this face
(extrapolist in three)
young framed worlds

retaliate by number
nine wests each
kind of water
hitched to quince

rinsed fractions lean
open to one
numb shoulder (kind)
latchkey and such

pi ripens outward
Atlantide inspects types
and infant tête-
à-tête cradle

leap trim toward
radical insect pose
finessed divisibly against
a modled fresco

ad infinitum snug
fit of key
dry ice cleaves
orchises from spine

guns kept leavened
unpin tiffs from
his and her
explosives not expletives

arched foot rain
bowing at chalkboard
orangery as facade
at river's end

adaptive river board
bow and all
sheds within range
fascia to chalk

midrange accommodates *et*
tu with ease
melody prepares levee
strength in zeros

watch eggs sit
in rows eggs
unprepared just here
and there found

everywhere incubating *is*
facsimile grade A
leche (weeds) that
dock to hide

resolve and parched
wind drawn young
weeds still hidden
from the glass

prairie sail fastens
crop regressive her
hatched house should
she dip down

rarin' to tense
up post latched
entryway dip down
through the sieve

fishing out a
copse from thunder's
mouth sleep on
claro would you

liftoff strains these
occipital effects of
rain by clear
and measurable standards

happiness breaks us
live to transgress
egress of vestige
and hack hour

our gist agreed
upon amounts to
hacked happiness reeking
with guess work

over the wall
and wielding the
neolith speaking of
salacious obstacle as

climbed or seen
through peaking upon
spectacular vistas no
longer walled apart

cornered will wait
for three plus
one mackerel verge
a vaulted ceiling

feeling the pinch
rinsed by plus
course of action
one riffs corners

drift they pull
punches through mud
percolate whole inactive
amphibious *I am*

revved minus sugar
plussed sans non
removed for civvies
calked to sun

amplexus grip ruptures
at blade's rich
bend blinking their
eagerness too shallow

pierced chaste yet
tinctured real as
sure ladles dip
shale thin next

in the book
of sunlight drawn
castoff square inch
field facing seed

locked color tastes
like aspiration looking
twice toward lasting
faces left afield

once upon never
overnight race for
rocks inflated by
three sewn into

fall to three
upon strewn nest
sequestered amid images
sewn into context

weight of snow
rudely awakened cart
coal stains thinking
theriomorphic as crime

silverware usually kept
apart from rust
that weighs what
coal would now

by *coniunctio* see
all the children
at work in
biorhythms as night

f/light stays hum
quilting to dream
open takes together
as work comes

closure cozies up
where growing knocks
merci splits off
period/ic better yet

to tempt sea
shade and sip
mead lit by
joy full stop

blue pent up
bids the rip
tide blind to
pond or ploy

decision tables rid
the boy of
lindy hop and
yon tuned finds

precision cut out
of luck trace
high does well
seven on seven

braced for luck
the septic high
does well with
seven cutouts prone

stasis not waste
datum not pneuma
conjecture is cured
disjuncta by ending

uranium less mentioned
leaves objection free
floating and disjunct
in part static

ripe loquat primitives
spelled versus spared
bloated adjunct to
whom they send

veracity qua dais
quo vadis speech
low to sparse
ground to cover

beside oneself lila
(no c) for
you are she
who lies among

wild reeds playthings
sole from fresh
bluesky wanderish stream
of delicious and

mortified by this
irrational recurrence of
Corningware flags and
down sentiment vine

canary parse aligns
with national pre
supposed tacit vested
down curtsey time

in sickle or
sphere a tribe
homologous to its
tact changing thirst

chance paves centuries
spherical by selves
and fickle too
with quivered tactic

take refuge in
where we would
have safely swooned
between two indefinites

more confidences shared
with pagination forethought
as kindling approached
from various shelves

vote of non-binding
promises to fake
out your coded
breath in smoke

lake improvisations shy
blue to behold
as code premises
breathing out takes

the imprint go-along
merriment is held
in joint account
lung paradox to

allegro on point
counts in primavera
chanting sung to
a sustained cadence

arousal shrine delay
waves off its
off-road sanctuary for
sunglass accretion in

angst may lift
sine wave singular
of pure resemblance
this young shrine

of aster and
cherry blossom fleck
sum of unknown
parts expedient upper

calm pending flocks
of hubris gone
now to unknown
source of bliss

held at bay
longer than trees
fenced oblivion poses
no-thing underneath but

fenced places brought
to life by
living a pose
longer than shadows

conducive an area
spring locks mention
time skips air
barricaded in being

west of something
flies qualitative breath
to be absorbed
into the young

finestra easterly as
knelt down branches
in discovery yet
new gill of

low points join
in segments still
shy of infinity
long overdue where

flakes written for
quincunx of trail
whatever wants you
squares off blame

exact wants fare
far better than
lakefront it is
written into ridges

motile or entrapped
a leathering takes
precedent the yawl
fleeced in sternpost

forwarding as before
all urgency propels
the leather sprung
from weathered stasis

forward marks forefront
pall spars with
mesocosm and scotch
quarterlink requited without

hereto*forte* winter slides
styled into Nova
Scotia cosmic as
quarter mile per

la corrida can't
be bothered grouped
icelandic first of
six by pardon

largo nests *aqui*
and other wise
played silhouettes recede
into the margins

health and human
furnace the staple
alli roots twin
themselves what's wrong

winsome other taps
guided tour prone
to weal and
manned young twelve

surviving only venerāre
segway into drone
fealty regularizes the
probable side before

regular shrill roundelay
paces the depth
in regular four
four time unless

effect divides occupancy
lightning blows through
everglade consulate *no*
loitering complicates race

of temperate so
temperament consoling ever
glad ragged personage
lui-meme afforded

tapioca acclimated to
same old same
aggravates gravity that
claims effete style

while the whisper
of a texture
moves the text
once solo by

the off chance
ground steers itself
next week abalone
brightly happens to

look at shimmer
derive from selves
plenary light round
apt prompt chance

mother-of-pearl
looking over your
derivation of self
down one interval

platitudes lack latitude
elfin range detached
from deprivation our
good pearl-toned looks

the palanquin girl
offered here eyes
stiff as larchwood
heavy with windows

arches back width
stoically to lurch
proof heave ho
dissonance on track

alfresco as zenith
where hoofprint light
on evidence thwarts
the Southern Ocean

Ithaca brims with
print notation warts
and all oceanic
or heresaid slight

feeling worse again
worth vintage stops
starts stalls trips
up panders to

accordion pleat sedentary
fold all ripped
per se and
landing on felt

torn interfused with
tear salt dark
as ten snared
extrapolations any second

metronomic one one
one one trapping
fuses ear felt
raring and all

rocking back end
arrow first wail
still puce rampion
root agreeable yes

say the pines
remain a shadow
blue to green
blur our walking

in situ fabricates
a running from
trois frères gone
gravid belly bluing

planet with new
rumblings fabric coated
in three sittings
father son holy

stare accelerates *festum*
adds or refuses
rhomboid patterned after
a jeweled radius

pling goes estuary
sprawl goes seashore
raw hewn boy
holds on unfused

sui generis thought
squint trawls sand
straw sings cause
for winded fusion

elusive reams of
paired comparisons flung
inward offers proxy
status winging *ought*

scant preening fraught
tipped astral traps
flax brightener plus
codeine burns frigid

gin in urns
surpasses rapt attention
and the lax
assemblage of equals

furtive ago at
la cage aux
creek crest slows
later will latch

wind will find
practice shaping creek
light low at
spaced time castling

checks gambit for
mate seducing moves
sayonara less sublime
the diadem prowls

replenishing the color
of lectern limits
quadrangle and core
as bit parts

quench degree and
jostling dent transitive
in trenchant store
differentiates type mass

torrents of need
spritzed open and
back transit just
wenchless by degree

parapet adversely near
damp metals where
baited with stone
grand opening steps

ear trumpet tones
pedestrian petals here
one upping ranch
verse tangents practical

flagellum of sunbolt
thruway pendant pulls
herd mentality tracing
fractured as film

it is finished
bliss gone mental
ratchets up fractions
limiting the way

cut cord vehicle
docked at stalemate
patch me afterward
more like request

do the wheels
ward off static
quest toward posture
following this patch

work west imburse
yin aspirant I
grail paramount to
speak now forget

no aspirin can
tamp the railing
that will peak
west of work

agitate the face
marl figure eight
accuse the construct
pause to identify

who accounts for
what face laws
fly home in
agitated wing span

alight dear aquiline
nether populace peaks
motiva brand name
marabou reposes in

palabras entonces vie
with me all
lacy tip top
ether's vatic wholesale

bars *corazón* entrant
lavage self against
as needed basis
area code lacing

tell me stories
of living gain
seeding ages onefold
as recessive ode

roebuck garden I'm
fine thank graphic
bevy of my
born thin redundancy

sear the skin
filmography impacts or
dunder a mismatched
space accorded cackling

cracks mist over
celsius agog screens
spry hatchling night
out of bounds

fright's a frisson
of a song
belonging to inbound
reticule this long

cautionary achtung role
trots the diatribe
on sliding scale
increment reaps yarn

from foresworn ram
shack diastole remainders
lingering where limber
face offs vest

magnolia bolt action
pisces caught hording
feature endures as
printed rain coats

creature compost or
fact distortion equally
fish tank traction
not aimlined oats

we have heard
entrains oasis to
manipulate azure toward
full figurement human

here am certain
here go figurines
man ear train
we pull from

clay a hereness
thereness fortified *deśī*
days she clung
to cultivate a

weight breathes upon
earth lures this
lay by of
a weak heart

valve gluts foyer
unguent or aortic
opaque as frame
whose version is

ramshackle packing crates
cover thin voice
splintered valve reverses
talk not soothing

vox exposure silo's
cote returns furies
through cult and
obedient *rex* metro

kingfisher facsimiles expose
coteries around appearance
of cult figures
playing stick ball

piñata modular resounding
avows protecting if
blood quits its
game genus loathes

inside information quits
the genome for
loafing *op cit*
mentionable in context

open the saurian
scales minister to
the unsayable peat
bed of bulls

callous sinister voice
chafes head shots
bullish paid in
full and cryptic

brays at safeway
flattering may still
occasionally be glad
doused while with

outer banks lit
flat doors rayless
walk out and
the sole occasion

fructose of wasp
bark worse than
trachea traded for
dawn one morning

either feather or
sweet versus bark
awl toned climbed
track toward mourning

contagion cages the
last step forward
mutably where front
extols the grieving

Ezekiel or diamonds
frost or wheat
the pebbles crowding
one jar another

whose brother raises
a stone over
conundrum of vocal
allowance shy proviso

caloric stemming of
this moment to
another tone allows
provisional reverse neglect

dietary not diversion
in ultrasound adds
roaming charge to
lobe's afflicted birth

math supports sustains
take out afflictions
sound out words
diverting evening yes

humble no but
winds are relative
seaboard retires all
soon enough festive

give or take
progress backward emulates
a register you
cannot feel elements

cave full of
*ave*s while eaves
trigger new rain
that registers givens

mounting bas-relief in
garb led strife
aging sacrificial finding
dresses change apart

win time host
temporal system led
apart stretches partially
healed while pressing

iniquitous habit of
suppression span dealt
delphinium clamping *shush*
down on quicktime

levitate what morning
is immersed in
retrospection non-existent
although this this

subpar tell-all turns
archival beware of
melody on atropos
to be honest

turn away from
wares valued at
melody threshing breezeward
seeking fractions spaced

closer windows bolster
atoll (at all)
qualm's odds and
ends two-thirds against

coral core breathmarks
to be alms
for the indelibly
rich at close

range concedes regulation
forswears the winning
blend of delicacy
and carbon internment

feigned sendoffs splinter
fragile personality mussed
open by inducement
like this flower

scuffed she arraigns
vertebrate order (magic)
appellation paraded out
mirame the passerine

show time Pell
Grant outcry rind
vowel duly knighted
and simulacra kept

at arm's length
macro bon vivant
restore the integral
study laconic vault

as if kismet
equaled choice or
the beneficent blue
sky lost track

of freesia walk
native coping which
way the cerule
scope slips into

fragrance recollected in
birth wire coiled
skills amid soft
land beneath smooth

pasturage aglint most
gracious gest a
radial *eau de*
floats the offending

dial water for
flotation fending off
lingua franca once
the gratitude elapses

next in line
eloquence of promise
accurate as aphrodisiac
leg over railing

overboard synonymous with
greed and mirror
furnishings to watch
has been exhausting

sty or cottage
screed globs onto
sternum's plot holding
guesswork over tact

in fact evidence
lobbed over artificial
fence frees old
impulse toward frottage

readies a pail
nets the sabbatical
act of nature
fanning footstep suffix

align batik revere
natural fan formation
stepped up fixative
to mend nets

haggle handwritten in
irritable arrival a.m.
arches back fixity
céad míle fáilte

arms opened on
fresh green acreage
for miles sealight
shelters each variation

searching spars tricolor
affluent spare lit
cloud rakes harmonic
teak extensor inswept

lacunae seep into
pared consciousness rapport
delays forsythia unless
fluent teak pares

orange nucleate from
portmanteau *sans port*
la fotografía bows
trifoliate pause wrapping

together a ping
less portable than
known remembered because
cleaving to range

details tallied in
javelin voice cremate
the missing you
arguably anxious dimpled

tail on kite
lifts after lingering
all ice is
the sung blues

let out elevate
after tailspin leads
ice all blues
as poultice lift

niggling over pinned
tones within earshot
loose shoes not
quite as enticing

staunch Vera a
barrack avid in
avidya if please
quarantines entrance embrace

local low cal
vis-à-vis
tines leased to
dry ranch lands

succinct precinct bucks
association burns bracket
cumpleaños talc a
cultivar means grove

happy daylight sans
racket and with
luck the tincture
will have taken

steps to sate
redbeat flinches even
inchwork will discard
grin here flame

ate swiss chard
then worked near
finches qua pets
ringling brothers surface

bay edge juggling
shambles shadows briss
coattail *prima materia*
garnet that brandishes

sir matador tails
radishes and ledged
there are brambles
coteries of shadow

kale greens muleta
tuberesque diligent there
inflects charnel watch
scaled back audacious

el centro hatched
now seems dispersed
calligraphic with uber
surface of chanel

auguries cached thank
remembering one might
conjure plot a
flourish begins above

anklets beside abjuring
nouveau riche gin
hampers afternoon an
owl toned inlet

tau cross germane
bin swift beaut
ramps down wow
white tref lets

ease lusted for
amps own me
others' eyes infect
the mane shine

playing favorites may
lacerate last signature
if one begets
tame domino effect

native amulet lays
laced alongside signed
copy of diminutive
recessive gene line

chatters *so charming*
the helical argument
abuse abstain relent
so I resemble

harm taint for
long term blessing
tarnish makeshiftily assembled
and then what

why venerate the
thread of roof
the caliber clap
travels meddlesome reign

liberation tallied furor
Venetian tumbler filled
to veiling metal
diametric roof rain

de-spirits door to
fray the aluminum
quality rebuke is
arrival not climate

pass the peace
ray is revoked
rebuke limning spires
minimum standards decreed

min drags max
past *porque* quoted
all hands on
choir residuals becoming

local cavorts past
future pulling in
specificity become ripe
as emergency handsome

phone home open
breathing lesson less
attuned pit specific
limits the blast

less is madrigal
chafes pacific last
things on penned
tunes still things

account for madeira
carafe scribbling Nü
Shu crosshair clinches
the importune chamber

forensic speech clinches
overdraft pronunciation
fares count process
stipules as new

series deplores *axis
mundi* profundus ship
where darkling leafstalk
sounds leeward dragging

hip to stalks
wounds ward off
plural tones darkened
by ragged axes

no sulking please
wind treats colorization
loss will appear
this dispels that

rhizomes hold moist
dust in kind
sans color just
mild imagined fur

zone of water
taupe caves in
relaxes west of
where one tries

often tao reframes
map of avenue
then reuses zone
within a cave

waved off feels
the hibernation in
opposites runnel inter
jects the equus

posses of passive
officers compose rigor
in detecting pale
rinse trailing watch

listen learn lease
pace while vacant
rounded off at
destination three (third)

conundra bleat within
cortex at par
three let's say
paced to lists

sattva as trinket
caps each corpus
stare let's not
retreat beyond pair

under the positioned
air vent grows
a knot say
treated to enlistment

mallow family of
soft exit floors
untie their swapped
drainage lie down

lure pedestrians to
rain often aging
if low flying
parallels are tendered

a clean break
attenuates the common
era 36 feet
open wide acoustic

360 degrees accessible
from here anywhere
visible open ripe
unto shoots oncoming

chrome trounces dandelion
stung roads meet
us curt as
drought line dashes

wrought lair goads
would be entrant
roaming charges apply
dit dit dit

point in gap
dredges the radiant
blackout grass bent
colder feet diffract

antiquity from here
appears lustrous if
slow within walls
each turning page

earmarks the pulp
disaster of byway
conifer pulled spring
into –zoic nude

ludic by way
of protozoa at
this distance nude
of excess markings

perfunctory *how is
she coping with*
those who arrange
trophic exposure to

greenlets eased into
via hose exposed
to humdrum prayer
toned down loping

zodiac fretboard tease
laze back and
initiate Odunde by
doting over sublet

quarter tones or
less revive ease
of hearing amplified
to broad backing

duly noted how
slurry that prunes
contraction also needs
dot or amnesic

runes cast leads
from a priori
laws felt not
recalled grace tones

hull yaws berth
red linen rocks
doubled bashful in
elated motor trend

clock motors on
ashen results in
earth with rays
torn without end

scornful trench of
bedroom basks the
flowchart solstice tears
advent away else

latticework distinct from
asking charred remains
to be re-seen
perhaps to last

lenient when bound
cylcothyme grows even
north south eight
years unbleached clean

lend singular focus
to avert leeching
nutrients in lean
years inward out

leer as though
under vert lipo
the insouciant rubric
commode of sheet

smooth across eel
vertical or mirroring
horizon through eye
of the leering

doing while undoing
jasper at odds
calm before invasive
cradling thrill scraps

electing poise before
a rill safe
although odd doings
cradle to this

tyke happily ever
the whiteness the
whiteness the white
finesse of pageant

witness from within
fine things shift
white to vibrant
hues turned kin

egress is kith
don't tell me
shift fine but
explode pith rips

plaudits to bell
tone singular listen
in to party
line reverse brim

moth eaten bent
rush love aloud
audit the circumference
exporter of triage

enter the audition
in perpetuum circuitous
also mouths open
over time hover

retinal filler seat
throwaway shan't lines
disband the perpetuity
mesh pillbox prizes

ways unequal means
risen from boxed
set thrown to
tines and mesh

thigh to wage
in comparison shock
lineup frisks obviated
truce variably is

in hock are
aspirations until closure
meaning cleansing distinct
from frisking ruse

personal matter (wake)
scarcity creases in
truculent dare cerise
flares higher than

crisp relo ex
post fact of
lumens air matte
ad infinitum tutti

in place of
solo role a
coy thulium cedes
carmine pink lux

oy concession stands
ole luxury gone
point click sand
so far afield

lesson one shake
dole out victor
embroil fling the
dozing center right

lingering victrola plans
roiling versus doze
son and mother
watch the embers

drench an edge
rhapsode salts farewell
thrips in heat
swallow tulip refuge

entry form resists
mimesis strand by
slim strand not
accidentally crossing over

border bars cone
estimated stars spill
thesis like outflow
again to imprison

one pill lower
than matrices although
arsenic lifts something
ordered yet barred

mated azurite crust
meso res powdering
missed call corrosive
fluoro spun anonymous

loud flora patched
restore faith in
azure as backdrop
sieve that catches

sender will scathe
chirp alarm incur
steep crimson in
goldwater cane lilith

reaping as one
curves toward endgame
recalls the steep
future of will

corbelled crawling anno
domini cornice of
locks and carved
tonic still draft

no miniature drop
cloth a priori
just the art
and belle reste

plexal drum estate
hurry now recoup
arbitrary synodic dispute
matata for exhibit

exogenous limitation now
bit mapped for
designing inhibition toward
next estate sale

tagged it-ness neoteny
sumi or face
level stress on
paneling vexes kahuna

meltdown for ragged
tender facing panes
of grasp texted
to unify unruly

fetching follow through
quelled gender drains
the expressions ASAP
solder the weir

rough rains sap
pressing ends means
computation etched into
otherwise young faces

slosh commence twisting
stout backseat disagreement
decays sendoff observance
flitters shotgun fortissimo

fending off hours
serves fritters forte
background lush with
wist and catering

to which blend
second servings abide
hasten crush oriented
flack brulé laid

vin number reveals
high rent sweet
haste second to
lack of aid

must read close
indulgence meets low
placed horizon felt
rails unnerve braid

risen pelt prior
verve averts loss
shinbone shine how
aid had rusted

spiriting incline before
hominid good try
for medium setting
flagrance *will we*

clinical fire spawns
fragrance at home
flounced nigh to
media in spirit

res complication swab
target the gluteal
supply partake indirectly
shred of partway

apt gets glutes
plied taken vector
red to art
tarred implicative zest

pat answer unglues
row aching with
tweaked brussel the
quick fix imperative

periscope aimed at
lake potential selling
to weak watershed
glued equaling unglued

apex of which
it almost makes
sense to cope
sample a bitterness

open ample curiosity
trawls field for
tension that brings
most pending questions

to nasturtium tipping
cure-all pint gapes
at wince ignition
don't circle that

plural flowers mother
planted in circle
area computed as
seen for breath

the metropole the
rural I'm not
clad let division
fulminated fill broken

polis with brioche
divides still life
between the halves
and doppelgangers lingering

twice the contaminant
neither she nor
antipode split filo
from pictorial washout

tainted pods mean
rumens no longer
spry failed to
have been washed

but to launder
break a leg
trouble with no-fly
information as contour

under form tour
of libel egging
on ruble worth
put forth here

sling blank at
name though weak
indices date the
odds of landing

even keel dicey
as laudatory ampersand
or else amour
or else slinking

proceeds quicken flight
auditorium *salud* flips
getting well picks
fluor over drift

greeting foisted thickens
early day with
derivations that reverse
picking figurative pocket

silver leaf stenosis
locket outcast woken
plastique purchase grazes
a thermal wellness

drinking silver rain
white tea revives
from mal refracts
spell of lockdown

paroled in ware
the mutual period
subbing oxidant for
rehearsal in solitary

hearse trundles by
one role complete
reality is solitary
though miraculously mutual

skipjack dolly fifth
wheel of consumption
head to toe
34th Street soma

heel to whiff
of *there* doll
fifth in line
topped off mantra

man traps arm
in planting box
courtesy a lamb
sheared with *frite*

iambs in box
punctuate quiet outside
the enclosure plants
surrounding higher stakes

enjamb starting block
with light inside
flush bans detecting
sutures are evidence

site specific lockdown
versus jamboree showcases
storied pasts of
densa charter members

assembled impaled by
épineux secure in
tamarind readiness one
passes toward living

cure for passing
live the rest
with sound all
part of life

selected at random
shower this snow
heaped on covalent
turnstile and fenceline

domestic now controls
alt delete where
predicates live long
in lined style

shift tab astronautical
chapter dares elite
delicates cotton longevity
pack longwave violets

terrain tones long
waves let captions
chap the edges
batted about metrics

scope of elective
avec moi clovering
terrapin cloth culled
battery of glamor

shell cloth tear
free with luck
amour also near
moi helps cope

in session body
opposed to the
stratagem birthing lip
frill as barrier

trill and sense
of sight gems
as light flicks
upon one barrier

all the same
all inquest stretched
dial up skysick
so much depends

amiable near branch
light skipping from
leaf to questions
pending a look

is it fortuitous
that depressing but
affable pronoun I
coroner of purpose

proposed roan pleasure
affords this incantation
yes to nouns
yes to sky

polyp a switch
tame the elision
page down to
re- invoke *volk*

lists of owned
vocations populate headlines
what is left
out rises higher

harp on nodule
dies to transport
being or became
couple highrise shaken

hiatus shrinks bookends
portable heights transpose
pliable within being
itself a coup

dagger or imagery
none as brunette
spat of overthrow's
dewy eructation (degree)

epistemic is quest
few and far
net cast once
anger fueled (pat)

untold finds purchase
pulls up short
the anklet source
is eventually torn

from once pinned
fender let slip
post chase toward
short young socks

made soft organization
individuals will clip
waxed layer terraces
courtier flung as

lip sync lifts
the song tiered
by lung force
organ courtly soft

tips stale monday
will be fated
hung jury driven
ground portion deprived

divided not round
still draw tracts
day by late
pitting one against

bonded devotee chez
feu (fire) spurs
musical chairs speed
date in scant

at hair ire
feeds can't although
musical east clings
few to far

fairest example of
splendid thought the
night she brings
stupor in close

critical mass returns
time space antiquity
a fiction lost
to vested integers

stone throw enables
how one relates
fatuous tired real
vignette laboring at

ability flinches rarely
it is labor
to throw voice
to a mannequin

on display tagged
pains each deal
or no deal
grade worsens whose

coherence said to
stop real play
reels in teaching
each is each

skimming its lid
slam dunk outing
lavishes consensus on
a middle name

us and them
uncles to ambient
youth wished for
over and outré

ticket of leave
running age into
sleepless intro has
stalled the figure

even less tall
than a figurine
in thicket pure
allowed to age

as seen on
here cupfuls fetter
partly the hands
persist persist in

what fill dirt
resists returns to
art of division
not a problem

to rehearse mysterium
save the long
straw will ascend
mirror in discourse

is a pasture
long of truth
hearse goes by
feel all raw

wheels purge grass
pouch pares going
stature of normal
effect living space

rasp treasured induces
dulcet voice in
contrast to pacing
justice for effect

quiz the entrenched
sapling of lost
shirt phonic against
fully furnished flame

plinking phonetic gain
onto a priori
lull gives ritzy
flair for hire

out of the
je nais se
sulk forget where
exceptions can be

frugality not with
emotion its own
ilk here sequential
perfectly wanted force

here to provide
bugles that fluster
a resolute kind
of physical act

brass act in
kind vidalia moderato
as a respite
glee in fact

ideal cento brings
bulb or skein
log entry cross
pike midriff maledictus

funpoke takes rustic
outer surf thus
ringing in lubbock
riffing on dicta

phone clad since
small prickle clasps
keyless entry cuts
message in pendulum

rickety tries not
sage lessen honed
kill fees inching
toward key stones

hit or miss
combing sand for
cataphyll and flirting
advert on tile

ampersand convenes sample
of palo verde
sticklines green to
blue stiff combs

honey yes casing
ever since looms
voices sent voicing
sticks chap ravine

moon rails choice
flicker upon vines
tressing the window
venting sotto talk

impertinent array kick
stand talking swings
back to square
one lower than

kickstand props up
wings are owned
transcendence ray to
rainlight seeping in

treacle crops laid
flat latency getting
over the reducible
compound help is

ashen pounds yielding
cover rope things
in composure laps
across what is

the whatness every
where countervails *listen*
kilted accord plants
transit in legroom

lilt of chords
lands sit space
room to count
history as veiling

jump repeat jump
the chorus life
blizzards of the
actual yearling cases

fife brims within
repeat signs two
measures long no
rest for years

foaling the taps
sting again and
not pleasurable by
far gone flick

leisure ticks away
or one gains
depth perception by
lingering this far

jejune obtains instant
access custom suit
seizes cargo pox
raiding cogless sepal

lutenist tox screen
evades yield go
carts tantamount to
reason lift custom

hydraulic skirt fan
base shine or
squat bar thrust
of paramount chides

scolded in fashion
lint and rust
will not appear
as proof past

ocean city *glossina*
solicitude as crutch
no hygienic outboard
under aisle scenery

genome for keeps
on board although
solipsistic tipped to
the half self

sparring with heaps
native tongue hides
charges its condolences
to the front

nativity brushes off
old leaps par
for the tongue
front and center

retread invoice same
shirt bleached coming
going if aster
drinks be calm

alms for the
glutted going fast
late thrumming across
rinks just melting

storm build extra
dumbfounds the pit
pilates strum checkered
season's greetings crewcut

straight across lit
by chance sun
rum run from
seasonal dumb storm

slalom drunk shalom
bottle rocket games
sunlight drains malarial
thumb out for

otolithic transfer notice
amicable retreat into
meditation at full
throttle wrung thus

the one hour
left on inhale
deep from salts
soft housing start

are key pebbles
the same as
grains of salt
stacked milestones tart

lapel or basic
sours the cutback
game over inanimate
stance switches surf

lack of latitude
confines the back
to basic saline
system of habit

buffers the knot
stirs the global
obstruction interim chase
hanging cocoon articles

not pecks but
plenty lanky haste
mongers flubbing routine
later to tell

club route pecking
order gentle as
counseling leg room
crops the punchline

lectures to gentry
punch the club
hobble blood lines
disorder a room

cobble together a
placebo hire more
arches oligarchic goal
shaken by galore

arch friends foal
taken back lore
to follow gather
round remove ire

sire in reproval
north alienates foaling
how will takeback
work through groove

gasp back to
lurking near lien
grab irking will
inch toward so

contrive lapse in
twin piles popularized
smirking where patinas
incrust the convoy

copper pure at
sky tinged green
the populace young
also with valence

as you were
unfazed patter VIN
number policies knick
knack modes of

integral icy kickbacks
held by cackling
partners fur few
chilly boned redactors

degrade sink proportion
yellow brick trapezius
missing reaction rakes
collaborator over place

or torsion stakes
claim on rickshaw
hissing across brick
laced rickety trap

knows to knock
for the record
stop 'n wash
picket led back

ashen licks correct
the clock topped
off by onto(logical)
regression not therapy

talked through seen
intake trips antique
top cleating brackets
faster than yelling

tell a racket
can last taking
rough equivalent of
spelling bees and be

force majeure else
peculiar noise nimble
honeywell of cruel
thank you dwells

thimble full of
honey rue the
day a liar
owns the well

crumble dull upon
the surface calm
the one alone
atrial diem will

face it lone
gnosis pains surrender
prone rumblings on
account of lulls

flanked are adopted
from a brokerage
hypnosis worn renders
ballast in fact

end erstwhile manages
to last factoring
page prints cast
in broken face

record temp delegates
key extremities to
facebook texts bedding
selfsame coptic curl

legato curls nix
book value optical
illusory or lending
mitigates cords cut

aliment soaking that
untired want schooled
say can you
breathe fake umbrage

hat tricks unearth
wreathing post facto
cool to tiring
theory of oak

octet advantage of
import verdure tacky
trifold post churns
scores first *wyrd*

vantage softly pointed
ports tack toward
ostracized or better
yet a core

foie gras grit
astute clay fixed
lot chipped direct
to lucrative pointer

internal anointing six
or so creative
fuses matched to
clay in stages

as compensation molds
initiative crawls forth
affairs syllogize through
flask orgiastic craftwork

older than raw
or fair value
logic rough on
origins of work

bubonic with shell
and spiked horseshoe
scab of equator
field hurried along

hell post pike
back sagging ploy
with shapely horses
drawn from fright

the bitless bridle
musk of classes
rolled cheeks and
tawny latigo manacle

husky lass takes
toll on vertigo
already manhandling bridle
after groom bit

puckish regrets only
forward the ago
furlough pension for
snafu as girdle

funds ward off
scion duty ego
tricks into repelling
ought with candor

reservoir breach cuts
grenadine best of
warbles below freezing
walkathon missing its

visits to *dine*
long stretches peaceable
as heat invisibly
sings through rest

everywhere operating on
idleness plow sower
enunciatory agape rolling
gifted masque tan

railings lifted leave
us where pure
annunciation grows to
every tonal hold

fasting idyll nor
ever null grotto
fussing after sweet
breads balsams prologue

5.

End table incongruous *apologia* learns its small complaint answers kindly *afallen*
themed tree isle of innocents white lie joy

herze comes later work an arson of procreational off-topic affinity with Avalon
moldering the hearth the retrieval the arcade to which again roaming charges

apply plumbing cost to euphonic lindens
adamant overwhelming on guard engraved

> an exacting innocence [she s/cares easily]
> silhouetted by a cyclic heave-ho put near calling card
> with/in her marvel of *vivace* holdings para metric
> chaste (yes, he-s-i-ta-te) before
>
> the ruby life of overdose considered
> fresh   dark   rouge   tea
> to match festival charade
> past quibble of quotation deemed enormous
> on approach of gratis face time

if example fails gratuity when all of Audubon traces the ipecac glum crush
back to flint and shower curtain chalks a pipe character in abbey's throw rug
loss column fanning out in pairs and tripody

> includes one drink
> with any purchase executive
> order concision of affluence

> [margin
> unearthed it's
> pleasurable]

>   to mistake a trilogy for a terabyte a shadowbox
planted in less dignified stranglehold SIGN HERE for hype and hip-hop
venerated bark the minor disagreement had over olive leaf triglyceride levels
where *semper fi* mag-wheeled *it's all going to work out*   donor appraises

> the neck on whose line it falls anyway
> vocal bruise expansion
> burden of proof

227

vibrati paced to weigh salt water power
  ruseproof   caves line out level
    beset with weeds and a gratuity
  streaming

    reams of ice   podiatry's idolatry
     whose encore shucks
      a ride to stay optic (my)
       myocardial fingerings for F#
     enumerate my fidgety quirking when
    the only instrument to date is : voice!

  why not box up these Nordic hoops
   and applebox (allow me) shoulders of this
      breezeway , cement // blowfly
// with querulous   concise
   repatriated **dignity**
   leafage repays signature of payback prayer until
    agreement is a lark
     raised to the fifth
      young hazelnut aspersion
 trounced by heat and handicap
 unregistered map relief (term
     limits put toward
     the pons of peat and thorn and washcloth
     less vitiated creeping things scaffold

    driven to thrill
    cam shaft berg
    turned pascal blue

      accept defray incite
      hula drift haughty on
      shipshape armloops
      of qualm and camisole

        alma mater to –
        almost diablo –
        closed circuit –

impinge on the burl chirp repress insom near

                    a-   ghast   might

paste garb on
motel endowment sixth night
inroom King of / Queen of
playing card appreciable *how far down*

                                        asinine chaise   break-up
                                        if they still catch
                                        the interfering call button
                                        dictate   &   lane

spangled   swimming

              a quillow taunts industrious goldpan hands spotting
              what will warm to sound waves and eventually
              change in the direction of
              desire

                                        jury decomposed
                                        closed circuitous
                                        intake somnolence
                                        disrupts constancy
                                        the might of systems
                                        evens (out) gradations

                    one hundred seventeen degrees
                    predicted to polish up
                                        the thought of Independence
sanguine mood of viaduct
the sprint of sea
a longing for
wheels temperate to ground
lo mein

              so(l) fa(r)   ruby feel   the Cheshire eyes
                    instill a farthing mind(set) into play
                          ing ing ing
                                        lard out-
                                        takes the mind
                                        and body tend
                                        to   ward

                              229

                                        forgiveness and
                                        keeping safe
                                        the populace
                                        not mutually
                                        exclusive

                    crank shaft over
                    drawn and
                    for the nonce
                    sequestering works
                    miraculous lines
                    of c/ode

cricket twin gore "dipped in river" who loves there is no overflow river
                                                              to love
No there is an installation who gives oneself underpass
passage to protect not keep or crusted
or Okay looted Aquarius pounce on hot deal the rip-roaring
stalag loudish where triunity is/was/has been

                                        surround diligent
                                        northeast extension
                                        excitable reap fringe
                                        line fits well ten
                                        squaring excludes
                                        me from sleeping
                                        tillage check
what hurry sings
shallowly taught
breath overnight
exceeding a test
cupola set topping don't Do Not
at the nape of neck

                            materialize expand into the life / living
                            thought-out requested tardy as certain
                            apothecium prompt denial insured
                            one summer cubit elbow to the price
                            found will move outside give trace its
dubious

demarcation   crest   kit

if the agitated inflames thermolaw
everything living tightening our body –ies
accommodate apart on the basic sonorous what's
saved free cursors directly address

regale the lack
of nutri cloud yawl
to quest for
lockjaw

opening in avarice
a theater
systematic flocking
advance showing

insistency equates to equitable frenzy in the mindset midst
demarcate solstice if and only
if upstaging appears
imminent

one's elbow constantly
trespassing on nil
rest

tight rinse
(love glimpse)
tender of the eye
port town
wounded here
don't touch

to be a sensate soldier
lockdown amounting
to concurrence
(dramatized) ilk
space heat slows
the lout feed

on the radio this a.m.
they called him *Jorge*

a(sh) the drive-by of the risen

clash with heat still
flowing

per omnia priestess
cubit scraping
till the s
oil
for over
f/low places location
well before the
cart weighs then some

m e n t i o n: there is capita   the seven people you meet   album

soggy at   point per   love-death   gadget   I am   that I

pin to   message sent   contrail   lounging   rapture   coastal

nights budgeted around viewership these million choice awards held for the
disdainful time of primacy spring tricks kicked out of the running door prize
suggestion faster goes aborted thin annulled puzzle if

you could only figure spinal alignment fresh sport scent re-dozen truffle the
dust grain width asking for all-new changing tick-mark benched or voted
down off pilsner bone age roundhouse tusk accent   now suppose
just once

general   axle   redial   forward all   franchise   headwa   time of

murrhine   and departure   gross radical   romance   the spread

acute   non-union   humeral   conated   and applied   missing

person
                    prison
                              principle

probably (not) pale
not up to whose standards
demand that promotion
the confidence interval of quiet   waiting area   staff

sit tight they will   be with you   before daybreak   the gateless
gate   however personable   three meaning winter   ill-prepared

bells and road closure
at five of   five o'clock   strips
tailwind from late arrival   dispensed   ragged
numb shirt at pro-shop   throat   closed   cart   carriage
casket   impassable   *lo gilos*   (logos)   thumbprint
until further notice
nothing yet it
hears it walks
it speaks it lies it does what a father wants

lard not food county not only   the escapism of cape merger
polished format   seals the heterodox

rupee chattel   to surface again
and proposed   to greet surveillance

tithe = sing   best man
    what it's like

wide open   intermurally
slab recon   as water

qualitative   but a minute
dawns on   wits' end

waits on   spared the expo
icing twice   inquest

calks with   potluck muse
flair failure   pail dry

rather lost   *media res*
in the middle   sanitarium

brotherly place   incriminated
trade up   his ex

bother calling   aquamarine

busy cross to

borscht starving
off the

groats zip
consummated

raging
cauterized

stage (lithe)
reasoning

of ask
trample (rumple)

you (pasteurized)
homogeneric

rang
amid pentameter (yes?)

from pass
mutt staging (rapt)

to stall
oncoming charisma

come hither
(case law)

safely syllables
erect a word

uno dos
trapezoid (uncanny)

logotomy
(for sure)

white blank

aftershave per
regent

claws for
creole (even if)

plus reprise
(caught full)

handsome
mercado (as if)

astray but
scansion lulls

not here not
(paltry) zoned

whithersoever
seasoning

to pack suits
the dizzy way (of)

guide one word
this blest

if this underpass
(were tender) lithe

drowns
home town (down home)

lower tier
glazed shore

non-venous
some leftover

très sure
tock

responsibility
lies four walled

monotonates if any
trance were (shapely)

all the whereroom
in a biscuit

anyone could
earn right (not to)

antecede
trumps weather

you cede
vintner's glowing

you fall
under glass

you dopplegang up
surprise she's sixteen

on my hairnet
blatant redness

fall guy
wore a camisole

prone whipstitch
in a corner

elope where
scavenge happens (haste)

current option
in a region to

fossiure a la
lap to

palatial
vroom (commingling)

raise pedicle
for sevens

clearly bronze
chapeau

merciful benign
separate text

to Act I
be they predicates

beginnings peer
lacrosse

violation
p/ending straw poll

stole
pinch of summer

fleer (practice
supremacy)

consonance (one of the good guys). Change of pacem. Glorifies the twice made
obligato when a throw rug hurts the breath. Booked as anamorphic

slow to stand

                                        healing fixture
                                        hand proceeds.

Derogatory one-off dips into amazement while the dowry keeps. Apology
makes north seem less like wind than craft.

Full-sized children confiscate the bother of witness (sparks debate among the
captive elder hostel waitlist) [cry to me]. Hours overdue

                                        take cover but
                                        don't look not
                                        yet we will
                                        tell you when.

A continent away is north. Keys jangle resolve *you have a vote* auspicious as
conduct. Oratory birding itself darker.

Barometer intact thus: infantilize the alternate ending

Shift the moon: where to rest a halo

Tremble: crawl in

Wheat coats: Aberdeen Township

Indecision: *better for everyone involved*

Masked ballistics: ganglia testing positive

Structure rupture: trying too hard

Latitude elongates: efficient as

Midnight: stick-on cell

Safe text: dagger (dragged) scrollbar

Lateral Oneida: pass and catch

Pounce: nothing but a technicality

Price: "rock bottom"

Pore: sheer excellence

Pine: model regenerates after *sell by*

Lip read verb on verbal: heron-on-the-pike

Will your opinion have to happen dampness on the skipped frame lucent
valuing deposits quipped? Perhaps next year. Mid to end.

Notice punctuation. Eight nights old, minus the onus.

You feel your rosary artesian water.
Treat the riding as assailant. If it matters
()revere()what you()revise()once()you close your() spherical endowment()
()then what then()imagine()hope as hope with e-mail()

> of course sighs
> says *why can't you*
> *be like everyone*
> *else* ordinary *and* plausible.

Temper hosanna where the rich go impish qualitative momentary slapdash
      thins to feats.
Slender whaling on a dare, borrowed *artifex* sterilized, put to good use.

> *Latex shimmers, or else. Problematic hiring practice.*

Why redial when your young hand must exercise.
React composing target the bull's-eye cocktail.

> Listen to me (maybe, maybe not): halftix amount to never
> having seen the dialectic
> row close.

Pass the lunatic imbroglio for wincing chapters, or
I'll vanish in your sudden heat. Triple digit do-over

> "this won't hurt"
> before or after

your saturday
scope exam
environment-shaped
degree or two.

I wanted brass but chose woodwind.
Examine the recognized cosmetic echo (demonstrate).

Let the face face
things and this face
reprove face not
save it.

Cosmelan is scorching because these stretched few daisies want simply to
waltz, vault into ceremonial indicatives. This paid announcement

brought to you by
white-gloved
deficit pondering

May I show you around? The feature-rich
terminology

rented chasm
thank heaven
redone interior
smoother curves
four-star supply
don't expire before
I do.

Accurate treble minced the top of bass clef.
Reading the moisture gimmick. Clearly, that's a— well—

She was my sister. Burden, imbalance, the mark.

{international conglomerate} {space-time coitus}

The pleasure is all mien. Here to thank, question, berate.
A lean cut. No more bets at this late stage in controlled wildfire.
Let me take

a photo of
[dreidel play]
the floor of your
[necromancy]
lean-to   lean away
[ahhh]

In an overtime not worth the heat, one fared better than a frost.
In trouble 80th deviation from far-gone colloquia of the storm alert.

Calligraphic remedies rely upon the vortex (follow me).
Local outbox collision and disowned for a period no less than, no more than.

Frontispiece the same justice arraigns us.
One-topping ornament.

Cutup or delinquent (see?)
Talk is impunity. Poor little

black sheep
wool-sick at
weigh-in
no sir no sir
none left
hormones
exhausted
ousted from
Delmarva
idolatry:

(x) three bags of use.
(y) three small hills.
(z) depth perception.

Are you famous as the innocence to follow?
Debonair as newsletter retreat, salivating on low 325° F.

Next time we meet let's improvise. [Despues de la muerta]
No, wait, let's just improve.   [90 day grace period]
New willows come to me.

Pillowtop card. Antlered cluster.

What a lustrous
day together   in Syracuse
The Place

Be a captive for my fenestration.
Aptly elated aid, working song.

Hi-ho Hi-ho
It's off to—
[there]
If sufficiently frightened

Cannot find server. Cannot phoenix the site. Plan for eventuality.
No loom wanting, we are fate. Differentiated and talking, talking, talking.

I wrote my timetables in Braille because you wanted me to go forth and
minimize a train departs the 30th Street Station at 10:13 pm . . .
and then   the platform isn't a snapped branch . . .
but finally "a wet heat"   *hypothetical*

Lodestar established in 1132 A.D. Gravity as speculation spreads.
Exacting as the diamond. Obtained by whatever means.

This year, thrill her.

Find your remaining moments in an atmospheric carnival. Play dead on arrival. Rev
them up. Retaining wall, a power, the morphine of stars. Revere, or if the prodigal was
the wrong word, indict.

At your birthmark the carnage of cranes, you will swallow harvest.
Pressed noticed (overused and hasp).

Aspartame tastes like minced quark.
First man, first woman (nightclub scene).

The sere land, spike in butchery, front-loader (non-deferrable) claw and road
debris. Endpoint sugared fact. The lottery. Ball rolling

rolling and *rolling*
and
hoping holding off

Toward inconsequence. Will lurch. Raise black sail, promote smoking in.
Sleep-away.
Press closer than an *if* with chakra paint. Final coat.

      Or cost to say we've been (heretical)
      On lost on stand-offish hood of germaphobic holiday.

Seating is limited. Sinks on the hour. Bonjour, one letter off. The sordidness.
Stall for tempo, rigidly as though apprentices were slowly pieced to practice.

Affair of our estate, congenital (genial?) guide. Is *known* specifically *whose*
authority. We approach, delimited charge, sea change of hairstyle. Correctness
lifts the state.

                                        Lenient storefront rhymes (kind
                                        of) with convenient lore punt.
                                        Brittle as A enters B and B sleeps
                                        beside A (*no touching please*) the
                                        symbol the syntax the view
                                        sideways never omit the 50
                                        percent overloaded next stop.

Ticket-in-desert. One could tape measure, send, text, voice the basic science.
Are you fronting for my obvious? Lob and rally to outsource last
communiqué.

        150.7 east   7.3 south

        Opulum's a corny wizard (are you game)?
            Surplus timer. Six seconds *gaming* suspicious activity.
                adol esce (horns locked) *sat for days* . . . is it over is it
over is it . . . fair, you know, for those involved . . .

                                    Breast feed weeds, okay? Or
appease the herbicide by association.
by fast-acting colonized

                Department of the Interior.

Best in nexus.
Next in show.

North of stow, three peers in a row.
One knocks. The other follows. Growth.

Companion abyss transfuses the banal. Hardy crustacean. Subphylum chain.
Out takes take longer to and towarding.

As the leash made into jump rope . . .

Go easy, go easy on . . . or just outbound . . . proseminar the disappointed.

Third base is where we finally landed
how far have we

kou trees

roosting

low groves

Unsure what to report.

If flux was pro-rated one might reconsider the gear employed.

Low pressure acclimates erosive task so it goes, fetches the log book before
there is no more of an advantage to any life, not any.

Under absence. Thirst abides even this weather. Putting on a clinic.

Tricolor the court cracked by plate shift, shuttle rush (minutes left on meter
muy bodily reserve . . . context *eulogized*).

We go [Vega]
The rh ere – staggered
To feign Deus Evictum
Consecutive Predilect Headache In
Emoticons
To pray *filius macrocosmi*
Our way out Optional Rehearsal
Of a communal dis
Function thus Nature Thus
Extreme Unction salutary Tremens

How did your uncle go?

stocked provision apiary like cut redwood

Was it the rinse of seeds?

goodness wholesome pose some before accentual

Was it the dialect?

everything's A/C perhaps what should conclude ambient

Was it a strapped condition of the pocket?

partner limitation   out of town   catch as

Was it picky?

catch can   *if you don't feel up to it*

Was it slow?

loathe   or the latter

Was it a burn rate?

elixir vinegar water urine

To stop oneself
effi   ca   se   nsitive

{missing literate}

Tragicomedy malts right
clicker as the mid-rest
seems to clue in
parcels and enduring
thirst.

What time is the encomium due
to arrive? *He's never been
aggressive*

Not to Knowledge.
Didn't Say. ¿No?
Le conte de la charrette

Vacuum set up in stereotravelsectionalpull of lustre needs the recondite Crippe
Creek. Can't believe I agreed to that dancing through playing as mother ǀ son ǀ
columnist.

Coppermine easymac for drivers who want to get the most earth concert *vas*
Hermeticum. A bevy (as) 3-shot lead (as) curtain call on the conscious lift. May
you outshine, find funny, saying saying break up with [be beneficent]
Valentine cult track & let's discuss   *hear her knock*   any female sensibility to
poignant indefinite   relief effort   engine trouble   crossing atoll &
bullpen   recovery of   shortwave diary   party to

        Looking across Bisbee one frappes on copper
        (mine alone) or are or leaves plenary
        corrosion
            define me: ford the gin (he said)
            fun is in your head (your mead)
               confine me   prestidigitation *crowfoot*   taxis
to the cult line
        where a rose foam gibberish points
               to the cross and several
                 intonations
rise to the occ-

        The tox screen replicates the beneficially
        epistic sea song

When I close my eyes
               The vineyard seesaws
           down along the threnody
             the thrip thrip thrip

        Parse me licks before I fry your breakfast.
        Blasphemy's the truth uncoded. *Play it again, only softer, cash*
                  out, no-fault dent unfixable lash.
            Doctor Faust, pray me through these grace notes.
            Largo moans low dosage (mg / kg) rosy turbine.

In a matter of minutia he was hers, all nettle and lyrically evident
and roses shallowed how we were when no one owed us anything.
Debtor's glance ǀ reviewer's comment ǀ shelf life fine print ecstasy.
Transactional neutrality would discommode each accurate perceiver.

Spinning dry valleys of whistle, the diver's weight, a plexic membrane, rainstick on black velvets, chapped, hollow magazine component.

When you read this book be sure to let the letters form into

When you notice quiet, activate your

When you reason with the sitter, tell

When you close out the account, revise

When you divine the obvious, keep it secret

When you clasp the hand of the uninjured

When you warm your house

When you verbalize the gift of primacy

When you lift the recent slide to point toward

When you endure the

When you cognate

When you rinse

When you get up to

When

. . .

Nigredo.
Alpha Centauri – Outreach 9 – closer, closer.
Evacuated, swapped from/to, swathed in a peroxyl group.
The dishwasher's intravenous
books neat notebooks— apostrophe | brushing habit— long haul

Th' league of lorries quirks
college-ruled drawl morning
opus points
land dries toward *perfectum non alternatum* mantra

sluice downzip and dowager contention
home overlong canary rushes
quite apart from cage
PFTs the *should* rage imported
sounds its *caw* its *cay* as in Okay
way of doing things into your
doing-in
Done for she is

all aboard dozes off
king of cups queen bee
Calliope capital punish-
bottom left square (safety)

push
the viables still trembl-
redirect steak knife *never needs sharpening*
fests this young
season sapped already
motives are motifs black cuff
or ready made
or gardens

And the ear canal
Courageous
Have some pones pony bottles
5¢ per return / supposition
The admiral will see you now
    shape of the dove
Incessant monody
    roused water
. . . *sniffing* . . . *scratching* . . . *digging* . . .
Why not incorporate the tuba
    intubate the core holding
I admired your city with the waterfall

                    Cornwall   Amsterdam   New York
            Relaxed
                    silent Eva   sulking
            low, low rates
            I saw debentures romanced
            For a change
            smiling Bethesda   *Thalia*

I thought about the *Hilda* of a chariot with twice the horse-
power *Clymenestra and the* abundance *a meal a bath-salt*
and I ruminated on Platonic claims
I caught a moment of the obvious retraction
                When you clasped the hand of the uninjured
When the presence here removed the trades
        diagonal screw eating its crested thread
From where the house would be
                            aromatic extract
                            dieting the electrical
                            deferens

            She was notorious
            She He the medallion of
            He-They (heyday) supremely caved
                    I thought she had a fleck of courage   a dusting
                    in that nominative
                    of her very doing
            Autocracy has queasy young momentum in its custody
            inducement (why or why not
                                chattel truly relative scale the confounding
                                verbation of
                                credit score   … interest   appeal

I have yet to think of myself as able-bodied
    cork of retina
    additive
    short-sleeved establishing siren-gashed belt identification tag swipe card
    Cairo
                on earth it is
                stepping along
                    up through
                    glam hour

gallows attendant
        friend of
    pang / epithet

                    a dictum as if sage
                    will wash off slowly
                    and conditions metric
                    do again apply

broth of boots and milk gallon squabble

(practiced   )
makework   shuff ling
                    off to Clydesdales
                    revolutionized by
                    phone for you

                            I (large) can sound like anyone (largest)

                    encyclo-wield
                the violence of snow

these elements too fro' darken some of free form f/light

maker of providence chance rebate
aphro- oarsguard *el capitán* a certain off-limits -*disiac*
    acrylic on plywood flats aborning
                    adjourning for the rest (is bristling)
                    of the good as well as press coverage (natural *engel*)
                    prance snake lock (perchance and streaming selenium)
                    rock-rust asbest os/us (operating gloss)
pare the lethal
fracture to
original b
one ~~stricture~~

        do nothing but
        accede (I give) (to) futurize
        plexor to knee— diagnostically
plethoral rampage acts (upon) the axis strung from

248

yiddish headhouse update
slight change of plans you have your
tavern face on striving to meet
2.0 requirements pull shades
lunches everywhere I cannot be

                  in gaelic all the ripcords start
                  to sing(e)
                  jump seat

                        pangaea
                        pass blitz
                        ombuds (aft on ignore)
                        improvised (her sugar decrement)
                        folded (quizzical baseline coping)
                        high-speed (reclamation plaster)
                        wall off (foresting silicon)
                        rivers and blinds (forensic finite forgetful)

        on the turn
        to you You
        you catapulted
        new times   Tintagel   dancer

            can't be good for him
            native unguent native to

                        nest locked down
                        turn makes
                        a vintage shift
                        to primogen-
she heard herself
voice what   not-a-part-of-downtime
                 Balzacian midriff sparks contentive glocken-
                        she's not worth

brackets tile mesmeric skeet shoot only the filled to mis-reason

        philosophy fairness resists (retracts) redeems (reverts) refolds
        (recourses) cur(s)ed

chattel (cattle?)
        drammed then dreamed then spoiled
        processed then canned
        then shipped by the day
        of night of morning of

it's a question
all of springing into
what-next fever
        I'll allow it
      Oh, will you

                 really miss
                 a hair off

                        reload
                        occupier

              watch this
              spleen-lover   angel in translation
                                snack glutton
                                nickname with
                                curbside potential

                    bear bull a hundred
                    hands at the bagged
                    arches *we're golden* stock trade
                    updraft *ange ingel angyal*
                    angelo gold meets
                    charm brace no fuss
                    neck on the ch
in *melek* a New York minuet
"a very good or beautiful person"
one stalks perimeter of parametric Zzzzzzzz
Thing-in-Itselfness uncarved paraclete voice
a chainfencelinkseriesupdateavatarleadrole

put your head down

essence

          sweet inviolable

ain
ence   minute
ink   perimeter
ies   person   secrecy
ate
vat   panther
ole   subject
                                     object
                                     god

pro tem

free of anchor
posse
glam

          paternity (sealed)

          vincere vel mori

long-armed strength gets you

quotable

contempt of congress

capital C

One blurts out "we are not worried much about the separation of powers"
except for the answer text of a bristlecone on fire

and another and another and another and
train noise steam a great deal on flatly affected visions

          period (.)
          grade of being | been | be

Where does *losing oneself* go | or become in the remaining *mens aeterna*
few minutes left in the third

quaternus
in so far
conjunctive   conjugates   the consilience   lake trustee

                    as a pratfall factor watch each lunge
                    for mere straits

there? here? where?
no path moooo-ving
magnesia and noon

            Open enrollment in a reminder of excitation (vat)
            packed   vigorous blankness of (easement)
            meager employment   menses (yack for)
            ejaculate   flattering   grisly (habit)
            unappeasable   thumb war   fairy (prince or swing set)

* must be included
                    (may or may not)   jamboree skeet shoot sloven
batteries are definite   ly   not
necessary for twilight zeal the very life of a thing   things   *this*
   tear-off day this
   blasé terror
   internally nationally blind | sighted

                knocked down

                       in a mint
                       delusive quiescent
                       malformed
                       dominus vobiscum

                        who's responsible

de faire ressortir les grandes lignes de la nature
         so it goes
         as it is in form
         formed formless

pretty park lit shadow or
equivalence sheer curtains

line a pensive
afternoon yes

                    we have a system of pacificity

        even a pencil
        clockspun
        seeping

                    foreground
                    as fact
                    inimitable lacelet seaming

                                joystick pegged in
                                to receding
                                halo

        staunch
        to gilded
        not much northing roster

                    properly tragic (look at silence for as
                    long as longing
                                in remedium
                                vault into
                                justice planks

active reserve
sleeps on plural
sill tent outcrop

                    deride if you are well enough to garner thinking
                    the impossible sprigs of trouble nicknamed lines
                                ((long may the kinglit fest of wrung hands
                                        ask for a pass   *how business is*
                                ((long may birthright sliver four-walled
                                        family-run   borderland
                                ((long may seashore weeping
                                        busy itself
                                ((long malarkey trim your shade plants

mystific *undercover* worldlings brawn feminsic –nesic?
shivering (she compares

253

                    herself to

     "listen to yourself"   canines respect high
                                        pitch (we con-

                         clude
                         done
                         form

          dominican swirl exclaims its low to ground loss of market share
                    the express lane's filled with
                    self-scan-judge-discard

core curriculum expends itself spends
failure to notice exclamation points inherently on fire   last fermion
                                        to leave
                                        phlegmatic
                                        seekadoo   slopes

       knowing !!!!!! known
threads of seeking hung down/across
gone
on/ov
er/worse yet   stays in lane
where worsens— to platitact they
                    swim   flail   reproduce
                    think yrslf intact then we'll talk
                    composing your ten-day routed   error
                    on the side of bold fresh
                    clean irresistible clean
                    side of   error
because we're starved
erased vineyard as well as it encourages
the outerrage outrage aging out of
b/ro/kn inauguration gives back
its witness of an atmosphere   vale peers into   brief report
we have been (made from)
who neglected to invent these stars (again)
and as a matter prized one glows on false esteem   teeming   intelligent
earned dashes on the back
burner of some midshipman practicing his descant   total   flicker
                                        encyclo-

pedic
pedia lite
-trician
   {pearling bears its baby names . . .}
  -trix (execu-
corrupt
    s p e c
        i a l
         gnawing gnaws on
         vermouth black label
         plant extensions
         reprieve and fluoridate

lorikeets ruby red lemon yellow endure our hearing stares
all night guesswork frames
the farm hands
land discomfort   like the voice of lakshmi amber singh cycle
       susan vindicates stamberg happy and altogether
     a tab choir to this vintage
        separate the syllables from sense of
        how made language prods already
      assailed situ
           interpol
       gape   disparaging
          pat-on-the
    *patched (thatched)

       cold compress
       cliff
       elliptical (endowment)
       featurette: The Injury
            The Wound
            The Five Wood
         the sequitur
         of sequences

dye-cut
   Ticonderoga
eye-flut
   Terrapin alley
sigh-shut

too many Red 40
colorings goniatite cord blood
         epiphytes blow
         acetosa onto Triassic

insurance / governing committee /
cloture sharpens plug-in / voyage
deters

mooring inured to
fan base crossed with
classic   duck tour

wait time!
undulatus   mortification

spike rally Sirius greener now
fist to chin | the brunt of

blunt sky would open for
acceleration   apoca-

A room whose walls burn eclectic with lye.
It can do.
It cannot do.
What is ignorant of
      slick embry
      onic (otic) lateness for the will
            (the) individual
            (the) breed
            (the) dramaturge

pause lit with glimmer (I disapp-)

                    merger used to be a quartet gone

stringular
tad monstrous
ravengirl at the balling up

        the twelve among us
        dried to vexing

                         sub-
stance
now she
angles for angels snipe
                                             whatever we procured
                                             we used
                            up / own good

               gardens (he keeps
       telling
                            me)
       erupt into potential   next thing she said was
                                                it's a sin   not to
                                                (fully) use (follow) one's
                                                (own) potential
       (owned by . . .)
       leased for a period of

                                   days set-fast lay waste

       what is to be done with
       sacramental petite vigor: chasten chill to concealment, poise,
                                   punctuate for potentate,
                                   slip, lip *belleza* off to . . .

                                   first chair sans cha ching
                                   amounts to second chair
                                   sans cha llenge amounts
                                   to third etcetera et et et
                                   (excrete tracks scents

scan shun peels into intercept wall spanning the sap
lings
              leaving pale to thread toned lines

                     now I lay twist inhabits me
                     who is it that I am to *reappoint*
                     scatter remedy backpack of the
                     stone heaps

parade

paternity
conforming

       this: in simultaneous . . .
       that shepherd mentality
       placates deranges
       tolerably misted
       beings cloaking
       hills

            whatever dribs contort the drabs
                                        you'll
                    hear me
                                        silo
                         annul
                  hush   don't
                    say

a word   not   a word   deny
leaking from the rathole the insertion

     pounce if you must
     hide your raw tail
     your rash-eaten feet

     how it works
     the natatorium welcomes your insertion into H_2O
     I practice and you judge
     this program sponsored by
     you provide and I deal in credible flaw number
     gizmos on disp-

                    (stop)
                    send you a tele~~phone~~
                Loves not ~~realities and creators~~
    master document
    in graphite
    or engraving *Vernunft*
    or on carbon paper
    or by thought
                the works is what she ordered

corking the palisade

unnerve
bundle of
corkscrew datalink
resume digging
or else

      outside my window a woman with no child is playing mommy
      with her adopted child and abate what is
      growing old equals the two I the three I the four
      alongside faculty
      of seeing / hearing / breathing visible in stall #

opus septembricide
yet telling

                        if I were you I would be
                        beautiful and I am
                         you therefore (I am)
                        not beautiful

but can marathon (she was a brave reluctant participant struck down
with the best (all-terrain vestment
can include the luminous (corresponding) society of her
strangely gifted solitude I cramp

                        at the exact moment
                        cumulated of-ness
                        that fertilizes the
                        unthought

worldvillagehouse (welc-)ome
elderchildtown (free of mercy masonry)
coral isle (correlate the waves)
window as mustang (you're later than victory)
   seed a dirt of spaciousness
on iron flame
complex organism   galloping
grave yet happy or if not happy then satisfied
and if not satisfied then content
   under a species of eternity

          when I see you I want you said the churl
                  said no one
                  after which, put aside, onward

                                        men over men backs muddled
compressed

                                        born weight
                                        women over women impenetrably as if
                                        abyss hued a crystal herniation
                                        of whatever once repeated itself
                                        through the human or inhuman or
animal

                                        the vegetative the hidden vineland
                                        verbal carnivores field mice
                                        in entrails of descent mighty
                                        prolix not superlative but wakened
                                        growl from acetylene from gut
                                        not effeminate
                                        recluse nor recent
                                        counterforce

argues / commandeers / qualifies
a vegetarian –tative actuarial vegan state staple of

            everywhere the exercise
            the example the execration
            of being the emirate
            waterless agriculture of what is
            not progressing as it believes | to proctor profess accept

else remaindered in emporia
empyrean downpouring
portrays a rough case
of a roughly shaped *standing before* whose juggled house
of unhitched river walk way to Ganesha the threshold
of a parking grid god of gods or trefoil
reforming lot for chariots keeps quiet

                        hiatus   millennium   propose | annex
                    (corresponding   (cheat substrate
            (vault
a simple deception (letters
from narrow circle (gaul pried
of origin to (fraternal twi

                              sect   *in the ordering of*   city
                              lives   *in the ordering of*   cabal

the husk (brandish if you must
seasonal (exist for tor
in exhilarated double-echo (pie plate atwirl whipnode
        exhausted associate (capture feisty laminate
        good show display ad (pipeline pipe down old charm
        distant third *come in* (but wunst whether not when
        from cold celebration displacing (repetition
                              nadir (vatical
                              to privilege
                              cannot be found
                                                    among portion
                                                    or discourse dis-

consulate *meet treatment in bog in elbow room
concord *handsome state chelated agitator of tripwire
willing contributor *so say hand-me-up defrayed perspectives on
                                        elective procedure

                      curse all who accept
                      "error (enmity) of the
                      found refrigerant   clue   course
binding

toast.

                a leaflet was let
                go after apercu
                bard preached quart
                et tu (brutality bonaventure headpiece a beast

frame.

true is as true   tantamount to the *hi* cupping *goodbye* in its
multiplicative boredom   tried to
ghost without light   (surrender

stipple.

these emotic leaving is-what-comes unwieldy
as swiss chard
                    on runway ((run away pierce
                    ambrosial chess

distal cheap trick ripped from classified
planes the state of K
and downward eaching retch a stew
qualifies [the] qual ities trade
mark as
adage baste-
to the extent that
        we were home
to the degree that
        meeting in-laws
to the invisible pretension that
        inconceivable, unmanifest, transcendent
to the domain unresolved name novel or station of constable consubstant-
                            aloof but casual
                            attired in the naked
                            bursa   wheel on head

            do you know your edith if edict will edify us as well?
            apollo lollygagging *plays on* quantus trail lifts rei*fies*?
                            intransigent deal   let's make
                                you asked for   and received
                                    behind   door number
            enjambment engineered furthermore assorted saves you?
            crisp tongue *do you stand thus* where it takes you?
                            forthright (B)liss and (T)error
cleaves clangs on copper necklaces the terrible
cutting edge the deadbolt cello
            questioning: 1) does it consume *Annwfn*
                          2) does it come alive the next hour
                          3) and the next and the next and the

posture.

faked.

euphrates.

bass instrument she chose water
glasses   bonny lass she was spark
feastly although matrimonial
indifference bled her hex

           a—storytime—of—magnanimous—firth

              vajra crimson omniscience

             all very vexing said the matriarch cont'd
who dominates: the turtle or the black bear
        spawning disputed sauna or bedclothed
           century summit whirling tooth in hook
                    hook in dapper
                    safe trip home
who corresponds: the principal or the teddy renovation project
             we buy houses carpeting
             behind closed doors
             . . . and many returns
who ripens: cement or blacktop
         putty mirror gastro-
           hurry *now and then* regard for   corvid
who views: blue horizon or whelk
           roping talk castrate for
             persons who keep namecold in a fit
               of meantime
who bromides: beatrice or shapely age
           lend me your *śakti* what might your
              intention gathering reinforcements
               wind-up toy on a broad plain
who careers: cassandra or belen
          falling down   each arrest   beyond   distraction
             before   cry wolf   rescue   marry task
who mows lawn: velma or three butlers
            in the kitchen with the wrench
            in the study with
             the revolver Daedalus awakening
              in trunk space with a stampede   intermezzo
              "all strains—feel their modes—
                 crossing historically— light"
          step | has it | | new to vigorous

who sips genmai near dark river: shale or keepsake molts
                         as no deed goes
                              so said where it
                         goes unpunished saying
                              let them eat

          land mines just about
     to be recalled (yclept) by wing
                    doddering jaws of

who lies about the stage: rep or cadaver
                         sales territory pulse hen
                              at the tipping nether
                                   sensation of circuit
                                        playing center field
                                             designates guidebook

                    in a minute the suspense will have been baked
     you may discard fears
     of the other
                    both of you may step down

          when he arrives, trance a little to the left
                                             driven trace
                                   and whosoever cleaves the blame
                              blames the other
                                   broken down though
     begotten from
                              shall live that feeling for et-

          and when the time spun   panhandle
          begins to lunge lurk slump into an accurate distal indecisive
          match, you shall be saved by your
          endocracy
                         you magistrate my mood-stoning-heroic-input

     on auto   pilot pilates pilgrim wait
     time
     sacked   disintegrating
     comparable   what a life is   build and go forth
          gravely   constant

n to the nth   always
      personal   *ablutio*   beaten into   spawn
          anchor   ancestry
            proven protection
                up to and including
                        dux bellorum   inclusive
                    the birth

    [what contrivance bastion slathers on is only
              mead kneaded finished at least for now   ]

Prose arrow the cromlech where they found you spanning *das Volk dichtet*
                          folk traumata land for I owe you
                                  at mask   espoused
                                        on location
swapped
                              the Mount   mountain top
                              for thirst
              (quenched of the
              all around the all around half-pipe foghorn maneuver
              and not no sir not
              dove mornings are languages in and of themselves a
knowledge
                                                    a quorum
                                                    a way out

This is not to say a place cannot be incomplete an oral stage a habit of
unawareness
a pathetic scuttlebutt a kingdom passing through motherland contorted into
epos   logos   and *obvi-*

ated
              let go   (plain   tx   tex
              surcease to quit   (v   vy   voy
              clamped clipping waist   (strain   stn
              with blood of category   (z   ze   zbr   a

The piebald swelter (are quart
The minion (called up   hard-tru   surfaced
First and second swayed choices: apricot (yes inf
                          leavened   parsnips

265

take-out (gravity

if room in
quisit
caulif
brain tread dark
the mist yeast (*ca suffit*)

minted zith-
accumulates to quick
s
and
-xotic

moment
a(i)rily
situation spec
the lilies gem them
only this
beseech
as for the quill point
daily
deprivation on
papel
who limps along acquires the limbs leap year
ends a child's
salt pores
legions of
domingo
as you   french quarter (y)our kiss
our one-way enthused
bow out of
sasp
sap
snap
asap

third rat(e)   rattle
cumbersome
relieves of sway (way over)
the deviant

drive (west of the story)
obligates the punt vitalizes
string alongside deluxe

cubic
fat(e)

albeit in a siege of diminution
walls go up and down the scale
heated and flurried

each of
inhab
slowly
downtime

breezeway rife with yelping breath

holiness depended monthly contribution   raving
into it upon go-on-up yields four   hospit   able   climates
square where trinity splitsong   tale   juried
would be (forgiveness un   for   gave   kempt
related to size   there   we   look   wizened
of suits   carton   fab   u   late   for h/ire

redwood collection is call forward
collectives tzedakah plate
magnetic

course of deflection

and the cause
relieved of
headrest

this vitalis
where he placed
third
fourth in line

you are my melody
my frostling pang
my caw-caw
my divination
meh   meh

267

a morsel amorphous cockle

everything I am has been
absorbed into alterity
for now the squall means
bivalve overtones

adobe or abode holds in what   corrective tiss-
I dare not copy   *nope*   repair is turned
into fields made red
with putty fine roll out
indignance
                                    (t

                              ip
                          fleur-de-lis
                                    badges

                                                                        ref

                    am
                              thrice
                                        upon

                                                    lumped

        in with

                    pong

                                    use your

            ~~doilies~~ wisely
[Modern usage] after hurricane truck dropping roof food where waters gurgle
up bloat and loot the garbanzo ~~a body~~ as extract inflated multi-talented
America's Got

helium readings bracket their place in standings dozens of *we deserve* hands-
free penny for your arbitration convert among birthday suit clapping fits   who
tripped and went wee

three-quarters of the centesis bungee injures your spotlight help request why?

how? ~~yes~~ notice the retraction not an acceptable flourish tongs rusted shut
price of doing   clumped kink in hose

            spray   first teeth
            103° fever fivefold

                              tooth as custom
                              pillow fight stuff
                              ing rings down to

feathering triple commune call-to-qualms
gas on but no smoke ever receded from your
madras manquarium textures broom minions
meniscus of cardboard display called out
the threads the watch list magic act
of second interview posses kept away
from measures of central tenderness
as all along the ivy pores go stain to
ward offing chill on buildings reviewable
skylilt crooked ineff- hewn ability We of the
rubbed atmosphere don't know the wrong way back
unbreakable implying something
through which overtones

                            if it is advice you eke
                            out of the drafting
                            hold your own
                            tongue in quotation (punishment)

"   mur mur   "
         (sync)   the
     mur   to   madre   to

valerian warning: if recovering from thinners ginger rutin or boswellia devil's
claw this is what people are saying about what a difficult job it is

chomping with less fervor than valerian allows
but witness this: curvaceous spines known as dis
ease crone over at a moment's
no   position   vacant

(peristalsis, baby, *l'enfant* 3 West)

been weeks going on dredging the 10,000th loss means jobs' stretch sails
corporal symbols drier than capsule is longest road proprietary blend below
waves Hiroshima and the moon cow

        to the fifteenth power dramatized
        enough is room

leaps over rich fisher *aqua mercurialis* sky central the fount adjoins *daz er in hulfe*
rehtes that he should help the sun not aggressively pursue promote from cortex
down quaint

watch that red zone ritual lift to power saving sleep mode

axial slack before grooms abyssal above recognized again journey to journey
the punctual terminating abrupt node power-driven faint odor self-moved
Ah— to people the one

b l i g h t
e i g h t w i s e
temperature amounts
F T D pulse
amid mentation

although the *izquierda*
        tame within this sizzlish clambake baccarat waltzes over to
        the tip
        of home plated
        conniving

who is nobody more than he she it | they them us | lines divide *de*-living
changing into "they say" [claim is heyday see-nothing frizz] which the engine
that couldn't merit ribald imperson ate its mathematical –ario bleak

        ^{tm} mark mundane raid veritably **glows**
        manners memorize

        mathematics, too, chip off the old
        Gilbert (six bald cells square foot

rampage one-away
will ravage the desert

apple crop savoir-faire will
glips tolly fend
for the fried
thighed scapular
periwinkle all
locusts tweak tan
jaunt quizzical

vine to vine forbidden *are you experienced* if not then gruesome caps lock tab
onto escape hatch sage brush— so the great great [thin air] greatness *was it
mentioned* an era lends pending nothing fancy calcium low earth stash 'n

> carry to cabinet
> cathouse upper
> east side prices

i n s t r u g g l e m e n t a l i s t e n t o t h e c h a t t e r

it's a   china blue **f r a p p e** coffin outboard

asterisk talk over sum silence scrabbled from within slinks off late hospice per
likeness one's own truth dispensed with circumambulates nowhere much of
anything

stickler's only
theo
ret herbally
dia metr
Leo form
sickle tropic

> everything has (in)fur ious pluck
> lapdance collide abet with (course) pike
> the fractal curative curving cure
> (remorse) stains straining the
> urbane Tipperary

the suburban willed its own concoct-
and papery silhouettes of carved
means weighing something ended
I hold these two
pass(ports) take me

leak the blackberry of its intel mobile work home slots chipped against anti-
trust but clever girl struck at intersection Red Lion and the Boulevard because
she never learned
to look one way

anybody seen my NOBLE hazard meaning take
a guess at playground parallels nod
declines the nomination?

landed gen
treatise locates small
mood of the indigo wound
quiet chi(ld) is it okay

being or else   a virgin well

a) sensitive b) hyper actualized c) trained to obey slogan narcotic

life d
rawing
clas
p   recursed
life

chosen from subject
pool blocked sender
emptying into

cheat sheet
molded spike
sown open-field
viewing

all mid-
morning he
slept with objected to
an adjective archived
I thought better of
(well) (sure) (that is
a definite) (possi-

new world at age unspecified

camisole solar corpus on bread skin
nectar mingle in full pintage
although morning treats
another morning like
a b(r)other bothers to

parentheses are warm
with you Petrarch
imbued with arch
what have petty two
in common left topaz
communing will swarm

let the air back beside the point   check up on
doors feathered better than jurisprudence
the muck *save big* on everything
throughout the compartmental Der Ring

Das Rheingold

| | ordination | | selves
one off o
pinion
northing   Froh
straightedge   Loge
as if only

credit postings
lied about   Fasolt   (facile)
this pro
cessual aging energy-efficient
                    nothing lifelong
                    lifts this squall
                    of trained
                    Porsche tightly
                    do please wager
                    the lengthy end
                    silver will grip

in tetrameter
what matters
is the holding pat(tern)

                              glistening syllables chokehold
                              of brisk you(ng) bird
                              thirds against
                              waltz a middle ground
                              deprived of corners courtiers
          hyped

                              ricercar bakes nicely black-footed
                                 albatross where it plays
                                 it plays   sit comma
                                 by depth if not
                                 by heart fed offal

thinking ahead
wise to whatever
it is what it will
or will not

                    render unto sir
                        unfathomable limelight rot
                    while recurrence dips
                                one finger dabbles plum
                        crisply into H$_2$O$_2$ daft textiles

breasted pelagic crater
weaned off nonbreeding dimorphic   the habanera
combed for complex and S-shaped   bonnet
sought after promises, promises
lighter understudy billing address grackle
flung shredded restored
suppressed resonating *let my people*
wan sanderling will sequester juvenile sojourn with
probed misfortune depose yourself bestseller
staffed at the lay-off
updated by outlook
taut as can-do obseq
          conseq

                    un quen (ch)
                    able lips read
                    at the swearing   -ence

ruses mordant clop clop clipper
cheat grass pleated front to whipper
snap drag plunket in the center
listen to your alabama quit claim
of a pool top shatter

> which spews (not sure)
> what else is true buzzards (rip)
> as topic deems crown stripe supraloral on
> embedding head errand where mainstage
> mainstay of motley

mute swan offering hints and pedagogy for a discontinued product line a room
that brings in lymph and bat-to-ball eye rinse temptation protected grassland
glacier cup

have you by any chance wanted to rip 9-volt Mu swollen as he walks
unabashed tinted nay though I give a response   none too glib   risk-averse

point in fact | fact in point | fact in competition with | *a quantity problem* |
flavanoid brace . . . so it . . . finally . . . . dies to . . . permuted . . . head-to-toe . . .
whose graces . . . one isn't prior . . . but there is a hold-over   a closet
a result

> *it's the process,*
> *cupidity, a hunch*

raked clear full sweep three times to make sure there is no eager over-the-
shoulder hail
last pass immaculate hourglass figure the common cold the heard *churk* the
whistled *pee-wit*   second try gone higher   the underpart

why don't lanyard philosophies go all out in the yard and bowl strikes back-to-back

bashful causation getting on (*come along for*) your fashionable unquestioning
wish I could unquestion unbring myself to phrasal   ultimately for   altimeter
the meaning [smarts] [*on point*] libation   ivy   sumac   whiskered   face
even paint's failure

> going out now and build you
> a heart cardium meshwork

                                        going out now and build you
                                        an iron lung the advent
                                        going out now and build you
                                        a steam engine nozzles
                                        going out now and build you
                                        a womb restraining order
                                        going out now and build you
                                        an incinerator fluid-primed
                                        going out now and build you
                                        a vault with air vents beside

        tapestry = the locus
        where she went away
        as if by form
        her father captured
        her informal mother captioned
        she a mother cape may
        secretarial good at what
        secretariat

auspice come alone and don't bring the kit foreign as instructions onionskin
warranty

                        [more traced than butter clay exfoliant]
                        [provenance a simple plan]

curve ahead

        repeat mood slimmer than cauter-
        and the glad
        reported form infracted
        upon heath
                [disclosure]
        I mean health
                that in all probability
        I mean amused healing
                will result in
        I meant no-I mean that I stutter *infraction* when I am most
applauded for *blame* what bodes well poorly not bad at all
                        (hindsight stays with visual ennui corrected
                        said the agent out of the woods and onto

the ramification)

we go

ladder-like and sore (repeat
litmus levies itself (see chess move
one last levantine (amassed
straw that broke (activity

it is in every sense of the subverted
in every lean quarter
the search is over
odds against
one can   will one   *hope*

for the Benefit of Public Well-Being the show must be proofread for bibelots
curiosa of *wish you were here* unlimited admission buffet philandering

heart   break
(broken)
repaired

they believe you were involved with a turn of events that anyone so inclined
especially if frivolous contemptible and tested for ferocity instinctually let go
embattled entrenched in

fray in lane in line skate *toute seule*

fair brushes against middling

maintaining rope burn dialogue redispersing executive report *quo* taken a jab at
wily waterfowl holdout pardon   my bargaining chip in I've been meaning to
~~don't tell~~   last chance   summer   wary   summation

slam   comp   greet   de-
plete

reserves

-voir

odor coming from | going to

uptake overtake taking
you always   obliged   without permission

                              eating down arrow
                              systemic frustrat-
                                    um required
                              at *shul*   flush and repeat

so there   who did
            compassing
there you   homegrown   compact
there is   cause   complete
there was   purpose
            compared

available for use
head covering
unabridged reminder for period ending

                    taking given dictation   *decomposed*   supports the
                    covenant supposed to wheel   *waxing*   through left
                    lane right life as the sequel pre-loads tintypical
                    duress   *waning*   throughout the agist free throw
                    canvassed neighborhoods hold still   *this won't hurt*
                    beneath the tarp and torpor written down into the
                    granite swirl walls is freedom   *a bit of*   domicile
                    keeping of form gas jet   *caritas*   equivalent to what
                    is within these gates the loyal
                    rush triple cast upon incessant
                    clogged box

                                        boxed space boxes
                                               us in

offer rusted respite despite the hour clang
from which nothing resounds this side of
that includes a mulch base camp procuring
and what divination will rhetorize the *oppositorum*
attract the needed nightshade
counter pull assume high-produce
to be revered osteo
and shapely paths shakedown

have been routine
ly foe inquisitory lowering each
time distinct from either you or
another you although joined
so softly lithely blinking
one reveals the body antebellum
in agility perfecting

                                    lamp inflationary
                                    lit with ammonite
                                    show meridian
                                    room accorded
                                    plentiful older
                                    mode of godessive
                                    whim astray
                                    cast streaking
                                    breathed asleep
                                    upon phylo
                                    genetic endemic
                                    to pyroclesia
                                    and refresh
                                    ment to colony re

                                            s embla   tiva

               rex imago

                            be home before
               chatter lull waste tempo

                 in a furnace
laked to down
                size
                    three is quaternal   no role rolling nod
overage
                                    remorse   why
                 to code a
                 gain
      advancing wist

                                    hybrid tectonics

free   cloaking
                              tonography   thrall
     leaves work

                                        indelibly dug

    for play
  recipro (capsi)
        -cal   cit   *ssss*

paligraphy rated first
in domestic whitewall
overcast shine
imagination trampolined
forethrown simply world
in the manner of all
copium caste runneth
each vast runnel
secular crank segment
torn stitch endorphin
fins where neck
sequels grave and
constant pray below
to play through
spoken for
smiles at

rotter
gotter   dam
gutter   ball
   spare
                  clutch
                  to nestling
                              as a pit pique
                        would save
dithy

ram bun(ct) ious   1¢
                      per scree

     and with

alleviate if on(c)e a way th(e) rough da(n)cing

collision courseware

strives to

end　　　walkage

appearing
straight-laced

singlist

"are you dressed yet"

"loop through univalve　　ver　　sed　　state

sit stay leash

is leaving in ~~five~~ ~~four~~ three minutes"

are rubies coarse as extra fare in or out sensory spats involuted?

crisp a-u-m　　shorter [short of] place time age
　　stressable calling out　　autumn　　combo
oars that avoid
pindrop cacti
will [with] no reflex
down triangle
to retention steer　　　　tap me
ever more than
ladle after they
look at the view
living pinched　　　　is there
once *from here*
driven medial
poised plastic need　　　　stat
offing compact
sewn Splenda
glad subserve
the lupine
reach sold
to
wilt
although
all-at-once　　　breathing
removal

this these
recesses

I wake sway trap
hawk owl centi

shrewd　　im

pede　　prim

treatise will
give it its (over)due
prequility
these corrosive roseate
inflammations
dry hook
line

order　　ordeal whole as

void (less clockwise
porched (intuit
refusal (for(e)most) in thin
king　　sleep

-ial
intellig

ence in
fore front
four to　　it ends　inten　decimals

-se
andante in 4a　b
4c means what evenly parts
caminar
the whole range of commotion

précis warms

scent　　rag-tag

to
"strange
stronde"

282

whosoever shall go skipping   imbibe invite   mag(netic)
-genta   will   weep   chase . . .   captivity . . .

mettre fin

spoken like

and the

advancing avalanche
rumored to be held back
mere threadbare crosshatch
woven happily gemmed   fireside

take latitude and square
it (not long to
scour impediments
the firm river sorts
scoops transists de
ports low-riding
flare   garage
(where is bound
turn back mid-
graft   baud)

au secours!

victim: white sky
cosmos

separate eradic-
Rx
he and
I she and
I above   thus here
toute seule

A Note about the Authors

Scott Glassman grew up in New Jersey and is the author of several chapbooks, including *Exertions* (Cy Gist Press). His poems have appeared in *Jubilat, Iowa Review, 580Split, Sentence,* and elsewhere. He is a past co-curator of the Emergency Reading Series at the Kelly Writers House and the Inverse Reading Series. He also currently works with children and adults as a psychotherapist in Philadelphia.

~

Sheila E. Murphy's most recent book publications include *Collected Chapbooks* (Blue Lion Books, 2008), *Permutoria* - Collaborative Visio Textual Art (Visual Poetry) with K.S. Ernst (Luna Bisonte Prods Press, 2008). A collaborative visual poem with K.S. Ernst appears in the November 2008 issue of *Poetry* magazine. A native of South Bend, Indiana, Murphy has lived all of her adult life in Phoenix, Arizona. Her consulting firm specializes in one-on-one executive development.